THE MAGIC OF MARKETING

DR ANIL KUMAR GREWAL
DR ANAND NANDWANI

Made with ♥ on the Notion Press Platform
www.notionpress.com

To the dreamers and doers,
who strive to make their visions a reality.

To every entrepreneur who dares to innovate,
every marketer who crafts connections,
and every learner who seeks to understand the magic of creating value.

This book is for you,
the creators of the future,
the architects of change.

May your journey be inspired and your efforts rewarded.

Contents

Foreword

In today's dynamic world, marketing has transcended beyond the conventional realms of selling and advertising. It is a discipline that weaves together creativity, strategy, and human connection to create impactful narratives and meaningful value for businesses and consumers alike.

The Magic of Marketing takes you on an insightful journey through the intricate art and science of marketing. It is a book that balances timeless principles with contemporary examples, showcasing how the essence of marketing lies in understanding and engaging with people at a deeper level.

What sets this book apart is its unique approach to storytelling. Through relatable characters like Aditi, Ramesh, Raj, and Priya, the concepts of marketing come alive, making it not just a guide but an inspiring read for entrepreneurs, students, and seasoned professionals. From foundational principles like the 4 Ps to cutting-edge topics such as digital engagement and sustainability, this book equips its readers with a comprehensive toolkit to navigate the ever-evolving marketing landscape.

The book also delves into the nuances of the Indian market, providing contextually rich examples and case studies that highlight the diversity and potential of this vibrant economy. Whether you are an aspiring marketer looking to learn the ropes or a seasoned strategist aiming to refine your craft, The Magic of Marketing offers valuable insights for everyone.

As you turn the pages of this book, may you find inspiration, knowledge, and the confidence to wield the true magic of marketing—connecting with people and creating value that resonates.

Happy reading!

Dr. Anil Kumar Grewal
Assistant Professor
Management Education & Research Institute, New Delhi
&
Dr. Anand Nandwani
Associate Professor
Management Education & Research Institute, New Delhi

Preface

Marketing is much more than a business function—it is the lifeblood of connections, innovations, and transformations in today's ever-evolving world. At its heart, marketing bridges the gap between ideas and needs, products and people, and dreams and realities. The Magic of Marketing was conceived with the belief that understanding this bridge is essential not only for business success but also for fostering meaningful relationships and creating value for society.

This book reflects our shared passion for teaching and our commitment to making complex concepts accessible and engaging. Drawing from years of academic research and industry insights, we have crafted a narrative that combines foundational marketing principles with the nuances of contemporary challenges such as digital disruption, sustainability, and consumer-centric strategies.

One of the unique features of this book is its storytelling approach. Through the lives of relatable characters navigating their marketing journeys—from an ambitious entrepreneur in Delhi to a resilient shopkeeper in Mumbai—we demonstrate how marketing theories translate into practice. Each story is a lens into the practical application of core concepts, making learning both immersive and impactful.

Our examples and case studies are deeply rooted in the Indian context, showcasing the diversity, dynamism, and opportunities of one of the world's most vibrant economies. However, the lessons presented here transcend borders, offering valuable insights for a global audience of marketers, students, and business professionals.

As co-authors, our journey in crafting this book has been one of learning, exploration, and deep reflection. We aim not just to provide a guide to marketing but to inspire a deeper appreciation for its transformative potential in shaping businesses, societies, and lives.

We extend our heartfelt gratitude to our colleagues, students, and families for their support, encouragement, and feedback throughout this journey. Without their unwavering belief, this book would not have been possible.

We invite you to join us on this journey through The Magic of Marketing. May it enrich your understanding, spark your creativity, and ignite your passion for the art and science of marketing.

Warm regards,

Dr. Anil Kumar Grewal
Assistant Professor
Management Education & Research Institute, New Delhi
&
Dr. Anand Nandwani
Associate Professor
Management Education & Research Institute, New Delhi

Acknowledgements

This book represents the culmination of our shared passion for marketing and our commitment to advancing its understanding among students, professionals, and entrepreneurs. It would not have been possible without the guidance, support, and encouragement of many individuals who have been part of our journey.

First and foremost, we extend our deepest gratitude to the Management Education & Research Institute, New Delhi, for providing us with a platform to explore, teach, and refine our ideas. The institute's unwavering support has been instrumental in the completion of this work.

We are profoundly grateful to our colleagues and students, whose thought-provoking discussions, insightful questions, and constructive feedback have continuously inspired us to expand our perspectives. Your engagement has enriched our understanding of the subject and pushed us to deliver our best.

A special thanks to our families, who have been our pillars of strength throughout this journey. Your patience, encouragement, and sacrifices have given us the time and focus needed to bring this book to life. To you, we owe our deepest appreciation.

We also extend our thanks to the countless individuals, businesses, and case studies that inspired the examples and narratives in this book. Your real-world experiences and insights have brought the magic of marketing to life on these pages.

Finally, we are indebted to the publishing team for their professionalism, support, and dedication in helping us present this work to a wider audience. Your belief in our vision has made this journey worthwhile.

The Magic of Marketing is a testament to the collaborative spirit of everyone involved. While we have authored this book, it is truly a shared achievement, and we are honored to present it as a collective contribution to the world of marketing.

With heartfelt gratitude,

Dr. Anil Kumar Grewal
Assistant Professor
Management Education & Research Institute, New Delhi
&
Dr. Anand Nandwani
Associate Professor
Management Education & Research Institute, New Delhi

Prologue

In a world that thrives on connections, marketing stands as a powerful force—shaping perceptions, driving decisions, and transforming ideas into reality. Yet, marketing is often misunderstood, reduced to a mere tool for persuasion or profit. In truth, it is an intricate art and science, a journey of empathy, creativity, and strategy.

The Magic of Marketing invites readers to explore this journey through the lens of relatable stories and practical insights. At the heart of this book lies a simple yet profound belief: successful marketing is not just about selling products—it is about understanding people, solving problems, and creating value that resonates deeply.

Through the lives of characters like Aditi, a passionate entrepreneur, and Ramesh, a resilient farmer, we unravel the complexities of marketing in real-world contexts. Their challenges and triumphs reflect the universal truths of this discipline, making the lessons accessible and impactful for readers from all walks of life.

Set against the dynamic backdrop of the Indian market, this book bridges traditional principles with contemporary practices, offering a blend of timeless wisdom and forward-thinking strategies. It is as much about building brands as it is about forging human connections.

This prologue is an invitation to think differently about marketing—not as a transactional process, but as a transformative journey. It is a call to embrace the magic that happens when ideas meet empathy and innovation meets understanding.

As you turn these pages, we hope you find inspiration, knowledge, and a renewed sense of purpose in your marketing endeavors. May this book serve as a guide, a companion, and a spark for your own magical journey in the world of marketing.

Welcome to The Magic of Marketing. Let the journey begin.

Dr. Anil Kumar Grewal
Assistant Professor
Management Education & Research Institute, New Delhi
&
Dr. Anand Nandwani
Associate Professor
Management Education & Research Institute, New Delhi

CHAPTER I

Introduction

The Magical Garden of Marketing

In the bustling city of Delhi, a young and ambitious woman named Aditi dreamed of launching her own line of organic skincare products. Inspired by her grandmother's traditional herbal remedies, she believed in the superiority of her creations and was confident they would be an instant success.

However, as the months passed, Aditi was disheartened to see that her products weren't selling as expected. The marketplace was saturated with competitors, and her brand struggled to stand out. One day, while clearing out her grandmother's attic, Aditi stumbled upon an old, dusty book titled *The Magic of Marketing*. Intrigued, she started reading, unaware that this book would transform her approach to business.

This discovery led her to realize that creating a great product was just the beginning. The true magic lay in how she connected with her customers and integrated her product into their lives.

1.1 The Difference Between Marketing and Selling

Aditi's Realization

As Aditi turned the pages of the book, she came across a key insight—**marketing is not just about selling.** Until then, Aditi had focused solely on pushing her product to customers, assuming that its quality alone would drive sales. However, the book explained that while selling is about the exchange of a product for money, marketing involves a broader and more strategic process.

Marketing is about understanding customer needs, desires, and behaviors. It's about creating a product or service that not only meets those needs but also adds value to the customer's life. Marketing covers everything from research and development to product design, pricing, distribution, and promotion. Selling, in contrast, is merely the final step in this process.

This revelation opened Aditi's eyes to her mistake. She had been so eager to bring her products to market that she skipped the crucial step of understanding her customers. She hadn't taken the time to identify what they truly needed, the challenges they faced, and how her products could uniquely solve those issues.

Understanding the Core Difference

Marketing and selling are often confused, but they play distinct roles in business. While selling focuses on short-term transactions, marketing is centered on building long-term relationships with customers.

Marketing starts with the customer and works backward. It asks key questions such as: What does the customer need? What are their pain points? How can we provide a solution that meets those needs and exceeds expectations? Marketing is about building a brand that resonates with people, creating products they want to buy, and effectively communicating that value to them.

Selling, on the other hand, is more product-focused. It typically involves convincing customers to buy, often without fully considering if the product fits their exact needs. Selling is more immediate and transactional.

Industry Example

Patanjali is a prime example of the difference between marketing and selling in the Indian context. While the quality of Patanjali's products is commendable, the brand's success can be attributed to its marketing strategy. Baba Ramdev, the face of Patanjali, built a brand identity rooted in traditional Indian values, health, and wellness. This resonated deeply with Indian consumers seeking natural and Ayurvedic solutions.

By leveraging Baba Ramdev's influence and avoiding traditional advertising, Patanjali focused on word-of-mouth marketing, brand loyalty, and a cultural message that resonated with its audience (Singh & Verma, 2018). This wasn't just about selling products—it was about selling a lifestyle and values deeply rooted in Indian culture.

Difference Between Marketing and Selling

Aspect	Marketing (The Magic of Connection)	Selling (The Art of Persuasion)
Central Focus	Understanding and fulfilling customer needs	Convincing customers to buy the product
Approach	Building long-term relationships	Achieving immediate sales goals
Orientation	Starts with customer desires	Starts with the product
Strategy	Crafting a journey that adds value	Persuading customers to purchase
Ultimate Goal	Creating customer loyalty	Closing sales and hitting targets
Process Flow	Begins with customer insights	Begins with the product
Scope of Work	Involves all elements from design to post-purchase	Focuses on the transaction
Relationship Focus	Nurturing long-term relationships	Securing immediate sales
Success Indicator	Measured by customer satisfaction and loyalty	Measured by revenue and sales targets

Practical Activity: Classroom Role-Play

Activity Name: *Marketing Garden*

Setup: Divide students into small groups and assign them a simple product, like a pen or a snack. Ask half the group to prepare a sales pitch that focuses solely on selling the product, while the other half creates a marketing strategy centred on understanding the target audience, determining how the product meets their needs, and communicating its value effectively.

Discussion: After each group presents, discuss which approach seemed more effective and why. This will help students grasp the fundamental difference between focusing solely on the product and adopting a customer-centric marketing approach.

1.2 Definitions and Concepts of Marketing

Definition of Marketing: "Marketing is a dynamic process of planning, creating, delivering, and promoting products or services that provide value to customers while building strong customer relationships to capture value in return (American Marketing Association, 2017)."

Philip Kotler: "Marketing is the science and art of exploring, creating, and delivering value to satisfy the needs of a target market at a profit" (Kotler, 2003). Marketing involves understanding customers and creating products that fulfil their needs more effectively than competitors do.

Core Concepts of Marketing:

1. Needs, Wants, and Demands

- Needs: Basic human requirements such as food, clothing, and shelter.
- Wants: Specific objects that might satisfy the need, shaped by culture and individual personality.
- Demands: Wants for specific products backed by an ability and willingness to buy them.

2. Market Offerings (Products, Services, and Experiences)

- Products: Tangible goods that satisfy consumer needs and wants.
- Services: Intangible offerings that provide value to consumers.
- Experiences: Memorable events that engage consumers in a personal way.

3. Value and Satisfaction

- Value: The consumer's assessment of the product's overall capacity to satisfy their needs.
- Satisfaction: The extent to which a product's perceived performance matches a buyer's expectations.

4. Exchange and Transactions

- Exchange: The act of obtaining a desired object from someone by offering something in return.
- Transactions: A trade of values between two or more parties.

5. Relationships and Networks

- Relationships: Building and maintaining strong connections with customers and other stakeholders.
- Networks: The interconnected web of relationships that a company maintains with its stakeholders.

6. Markets

- Markets: The set of actual and potential buyers of a product or service.

7. Marketers and Prospects

- Marketers: Individuals or organizations that seek to stimulate and facilitate exchanges.
- Prospects: Individuals or organizations that are potential buyers.

Marketing Philosophies / Competing Concepts of Marketing:

- **Production Concept**: Focuses on making products widely available and affordable. Companies aim for high production efficiency and low costs. Example: Ford's Model T car, produced in large volumes at low costs.
- **Product Concept**: Emphasizes creating products with the best quality, performance, and features. Companies invest in innovation but can risk overlooking customer needs. Example: Apple's continuous innovation with its

iPhone.

- **Selling Concept**: Relies on aggressive promotion to sell unsought goods like insurance, often focusing on generating sales transactions. Example: Life insurance companies using sales tactics to push policies.
- **Marketing Concept**: Centres on understanding customers' needs and desires and offering products that fulfil those needs more effectively than competitors. Example: Amazon uses data to personalize offerings and ensure customer satisfaction.

- **Societal Marketing Concept**: This concept questions whether the pure marketing concept overlooks possible conflicts between consumer short-term wants and consumer long-term welfare. It holds that marketing strategy should deliver value to customers in a way that maintains or improves both the consumer's and society's well-being.

- **Holistic Marketing Concept**: The Holistic Marketing Concept is an approach that considers a business and all its parts as a unified whole, aiming to create a seamless and consistent experience for customers. This concept recognizes that all aspects of marketing are interconnected and that a broad, integrated perspective is essential for achieving optimal performance.

Key Components of Holistic Marketing Concept:

1. **Relationship Marketing:**

    - **Focus:** Building long-term, meaningful relationships with customers, suppliers, partners, and other stakeholders.
    - **Goal:** Foster customer loyalty and engagement by providing consistent value and personalized experiences.

2. **Integrated Marketing:**

    - **Focus:** Coordinating all marketing activities and channels to deliver a cohesive message.
    - **Goal:** Ensure that all promotional tools and messaging work together harmoniously to reinforce the brand and its values.

3. **Internal Marketing:**

    - **Focus:** Aligning and motivating employees at all levels to deliver on the company's marketing promises.
    - **Goal:** Encourage employee engagement and ensure that everyone understands and supports the company's mission and marketing objectives.

4. **Socially Responsible Marketing:**

    - **Focus:** Considering the ethical, environmental, legal, and social impacts of marketing activities.
    - **Goal:** Operate in a manner that is sustainable and socially responsible, contributing positively to society and minimizing negative effects.

Latest Marketing Concepts:

- **Digital Marketing**: Utilizes digital channels to engage customers through social media, SEO, and email. Example: Companies using influencer marketing on Instagram to connect with their target audience.
- **Sustainable Marketing**: Focuses on creating products that meet customer needs while considering environmental and social impacts. Example: Brands producing eco-friendly products and promoting social responsibility.

Famous Definitions of Marketing

- **Philip Kotler**: "Marketing is the science and art of exploring, creating, and delivering value to satisfy the needs of a target market at a profit. Marketing identifies unfulfilled needs and desires. It defines, measures, and quantifies the size of the identified market and the profit potential. It pinpoints which segments the company is capable of serving best and designs and promotes the appropriate products and services" (Kotler, 2003)
- **American Marketing Association (AMA)**: "Marketing is the activity, set of institutions, and processes for creating, communicating, delivering, and exchanging offerings that have value for customers, clients, partners, and society at large" (AMA, 2017).
- **Peter Drucker**: "The aim of marketing is to know and understand the customer so well the product or service fits him and sells itself. Ideally, marketing should result in a customer who is ready to buy. All that should be needed then is to make the product or service available" (Drucker, 1973).
- **Seth Godin**: "Marketing is a contest for people's attention" (Godin, 1999).
- **Chartered Institute of Marketing (CIM)**: "Marketing is the management process responsible for identifying, anticipating, and satisfying customer requirements profitably" (CIM, n.d.).
- **HubSpot**: "Marketing is the process of getting people interested in your company's product or service. This happens through market research, analysis, and understanding your ideal customer's interests. Marketing pertains to all aspects of a business, including product development, distribution methods, sales, and advertising" (HubSpot, n.d.).

New Definition of Marketing

"Marketing is the strategic process of understanding, anticipating, and fulfilling customer needs and desires by creating, communicating, and delivering valuable products or services. It involves a holistic approach that integrates market research, customer insights, networking, digital engagement, and ethical practices to build strong, long-lasting relationships with customers and partners. Marketing drives sustainable business growth while contributing positively to society, leveraging networks and collaborations to amplify reach and impact."

Key Aspects of This Definition:

- **Strategic Process**: Emphasizes thoughtful planning that aligns with the organization's broader business objectives.
- **Understanding and Anticipating Customer Needs**: Reflects the importance of deeply understanding and predicting customer desires.
- **Value Creation and Delivery**: Highlights marketing's role in developing and delivering value to customers.
- **Holistic Approach**: Covers all aspects from product development to post-purchase support across traditional and digital platforms.
- **Networking**: Recognizes the importance of building relationships with industry partners, influencers, and stakeholders.

- **Digital Engagement**: Acknowledges the significance of engaging customers through digital channels.
- **Ethical Practices**: Reflects modern emphasis on corporate social responsibility.
- **Sustainable Growth**: Focuses on marketing's role in driving long-term, sustainable business growth.
- **Building Relationships**: Stresses the goal of forging strong, lasting relationships with customers and partners.
- **Leveraging Networks**: Highlights the power of networking and collaborations to amplify marketing efforts.

Practical Activity: Classroom Brainstorming

Activity Name: *Marketing Concept Map*

Setup: Ask students to create a concept map that visualizes the evolution of marketing concepts from the Production Concept to the latest Digital and Sustainable Marketing concepts. Each branch of the map should include definitions, examples, and key characteristics.

Discussion: Discuss how each concept reflects the changing priorities of businesses and consumers over time. This will help students understand how marketing has evolved to become more customer-focused and socially responsible.

1.3 The Marketing Mix (4 Ps)

Aditi's Success with the 4 Ps

As Aditi delved further into the book, she came across the concept of the Marketing Mix, often referred to as the 4 Ps—Product, Price, Place, and Promotion. These, the book explained, were the key ingredients in the magical potion of marketing (McCarthy, 1964). Aditi began to think about how each of these elements could be optimized to create a successful marketing strategy for her skincare line.

- **Product**: This involves deciding what to sell. It includes the features, design, quality, branding, and packaging of the product. Aditi realized her products needed to stand out in the market. She focused on the unique benefits of her organic ingredients, making them the centerpiece of her product offering. She also considered the product life cycle, ensuring her product stayed relevant and desirable over time.
- **Price**: Pricing determines how much customers will pay for the product. Pricing isn't just about covering costs and making a profit; it's also about conveying value. Aditi wanted her products to be perceived as premium, but she also didn't want to price them out of reach for her target audience. She decided on a pricing strategy that struck a balance, offering value for money while reinforcing the product's high quality.
- **Place**: This refers to how the product is distributed and where it is available for purchase. Effective distribution ensures the product is available where and when customers want it, enhancing the customer's buying experience. **Indian Industry Example**: Nestlé's Maggi is a great example of a company that has mastered the "Place" aspect of the marketing mix. Maggi is available in nearly every grocery store across India, from the largest supermarkets in metropolitan cities to the smallest kirana shops in remote villages. Nestlé's extensive distribution network ensures Maggi is accessible to all segments of the Indian population, making it a household name and a staple in Indian kitchens.
- **Promotion**: Promotion involves communicating the benefits of the product to potential customers. It includes advertising, public relations, sales promotions, and other marketing tactics. Aditi knew she needed to build awareness of her brand and educate consumers about the benefits of her products. She devised a promotional strategy that included social media marketing, collaborations with beauty influencers, and participating in local fairs to reach her audience.

Can You Change the Sequence?

While the 4 Ps are typically discussed in a particular order, their sequence can sometimes be adjusted based on the business context. However, changing the sequence must be done thoughtfully, as the elements are interconnected.

Example: Tata Nano

The Tata Nano is a well-known example of how the sequence of the 4 Ps can significantly impact a product's success.

- **Price**: The Tata Nano was conceived as the world's cheapest car, priced at ₹1 lakh. This price point was the primary driver for the entire project. The goal was to make car ownership accessible to millions of Indians who could otherwise only afford two-wheelers. However, focusing on price as the starting point led to significant challenges in the other Ps.
- **Product**: To meet the aggressive pricing target, compromises had to be made in the car's design and features. While the Nano was innovative in many ways—like its lightweight body, efficient fuel consumption, and compact design—it was perceived as too basic. The car was stripped down to essentials, which included a smaller engine, lower build quality, and minimalistic interior features. Over time, Tata Motors did attempt to add more features and variants to the Nano, but the initial perception of it being a "cheap" car persisted.
- **Place**: The distribution of the Nano was initially well-planned with a strong dealership network. However, after the relocation of the manufacturing plant from Singur, West Bengal, to Sanand, Gujarat, due to political issues, there were delays and production challenges. This impacted the timely availability of the car and added to the overall production costs.
- **Promotion**: The promotion of the Nano focused heavily on its affordability, branding it as "the people's car." However, this created a perception problem. In India, car ownership is often seen as a status symbol, and the Nano's positioning as the cheapest car led many potential buyers to avoid it, fearing it would reflect poorly on their social standing.

Outcome: The Tata Nano struggled in the market because the initial focus on Price dictated the Product's limitations. Over time, the costs of production increased due to inflation and rising input costs, making it impossible to maintain the ₹1 lakh price point. The perception issues, compounded by the minimalistic design and features, meant that even when Tata Motors tried to introduce upgraded versions of the Nano, it was difficult to change the market's perception of the car.

Practical Activity: Classroom Workshop

Activity Name: *The Marketing Mix Potion*

Setup: Give students a fictional product—like a new type of energy drink or eco-friendly stationery. In groups, they will develop a marketing mix for this product, considering the 4 Ps. Encourage them to think creatively about how changing the sequence of the 4 Ps might alter their strategy. For example, they could start by choosing the Place (distribution channels) first if they believe it will drive other decisions.

Presentation: Each group presents their marketing mix to the class, explaining the rationale behind their choices and whether they changed the sequence of the 4 Ps. The class can discuss which strategies seem most effective and why.

1.4 The Marketing Process

Aditi's Marketing Blueprint

Aditi's next challenge was to put all her newfound knowledge into a cohesive strategy. The book outlined the marketing process, a step-by-step guide that would lead her to success. The process involved understanding the market, developing a marketing strategy, creating and delivering value, and finally, capturing that value through sales (Jobber & Ellis-Chadwick, 2019).

1. **Understanding the Market**: Aditi started by conducting market research. She surveyed potential customers, analyzed competitors, and identified gaps in the market.
2. **Developing a Marketing Strategy**: Based on her research, Aditi crafted a strategy that focused on her unique value proposition—high-quality, organic skincare made from locally sourced ingredients.
3. **Creating Value**: She then designed her product line to reflect this strategy, ensuring that every aspect of her products—from the ingredients to the packaging—aligned with her brand's promise.
4. **Delivering Value**: Aditi chose distribution channels that would reach her target customers effectively. She also trained her sales team to communicate the value of her products clearly and convincingly.
5. **Capturing Value**: Finally, Aditi implemented a pricing strategy that allowed her to capture the value she created, ensuring that her business remained profitable.

Magic Box: Quick Spell: The Marketing Process

Step 1: Understand the Market: Research your audience and competitors.

Step 2: Develop a Strategy: Create a plan that highlights your unique value.

Step 3: Create Value: Design products that fulfill customer needs.

Step 4: Deliver Value: Choose the right channels to get your product to customers.

Step 5: Capture Value: Price your product to reflect its worth and ensure profitability.

Indian Industry Example: Flipkart, one of India's largest e-commerce platforms, exemplifies a successful marketing process. They started by understanding the Indian market's unique needs (e.g., cash on delivery, local languages), developed a strategy to cater to these needs, created a user-friendly platform, delivered value through efficient logistics, and captured value by building brand loyalty among millions of customers.

Practical Activity: Marketing Process Simulation

Activity Name: The Marketing Wizard's Path

Setup: Students will simulate the marketing process by choosing a product they wish to market. They'll follow the steps: research, strategy, value creation, value delivery, and capturing value. Each step will involve specific tasks, such as conducting a mini-survey, developing a brand strategy, and choosing a distribution channel.

Reflection: After completing the simulation, students will reflect on what they learned at each step and how their understanding of the marketing process evolved. This activity will help solidify their grasp of the essential stages in creating a successful marketing strategy.

CHAPTER II

The Marketing Environment

Ramesh's Farm Struggles with Change

Ramesh's organic fruit farm had always been a staple of the local community. The freshness of his mangoes and guavas, handpicked with care, kept the townsfolk coming back year after year. But recently, something had changed. The same people who once queued up for his fruits were now visiting the newly opened supermarket. It wasn't just the local buyers either—big retailers were starting to cut deals directly with larger, industrial farms that could offer better economies of scale.

On top of that, the weather was becoming more unpredictable. Rain patterns had shifted, pests were attacking crops, and drought seemed to threaten every year. Ramesh's confidence began to wane. His family suggested new ways of selling, maybe by partnering with local organic markets or even selling online. But he realized that to survive, he needed to understand what was really changing around him.

Ramesh started reading about market trends, competitors, and new technologies. He found that many businesses were affected by external forces beyond their control. His small farm was competing not just with local vendors, but with global supply chains, new technological platforms, and changing consumer preferences. He needed to adapt, and fast.

Through this story, we can begin to understand how businesses need to navigate the **marketing environment**, which includes both **internal** and **external** factors that affect their success. Ramesh's story is a microcosm of how every business, whether large or small, must adapt to the forces around it.

Defining the Marketing Environment

The **marketing environment** refers to the **external forces and factors** that influence a company's ability to develop and maintain successful customer relationships. These factors can either directly or indirectly affect the entire marketing strategy, product development, and customer satisfaction.

Businesses, like Ramesh's farm, need to consistently evaluate their marketing environment to stay competitive. The marketing environment is categorized into two primary segments:

1. **Microenvironment** – Factors directly affecting the business but can be somewhat controlled or influenced.
2. **Macroenvironment** – Larger societal forces that affect all businesses and are beyond the control of a company.

Microenvironment

The **microenvironment** includes the immediate forces that directly affect a company's ability to serve its customers. These forces are often within the company's immediate vicinity, and businesses can influence or adapt to these forces with strategic planning.

Key elements:

Microenvironment Component	Description	Indian Industry Example
The Company	Internal departments, resources, and capabilities of the company.	Ramesh's farm operations include his family, employees, and suppliers, all working to produce and sell organic fruits.
Suppliers	Provide the raw materials and resources necessary for production.	Indian food processing companies like Parle and Britannia depend on reliable wheat and milk suppliers for their products.
Customers	The target market or end users of the product/service. Businesses need to meet their evolving needs and preferences.	E-commerce giants like Amazon India invest heavily in customer research to ensure they meet the needs of a growing middle class.
Marketing Intermediaries	Firms or individuals who help promote, sell, and distribute the company's products to final buyers.	Reliance Fresh uses distribution networks to reach both urban and rural consumers efficiently.
Competitors	Other companies offering similar products or services. Competitive strategies focus on differentiation.	In the Indian telecom market, companies like Airtel and Jio are constantly competing by lowering prices and improving services.
Public	Any group with an actual or potential interest in or impact on a company's ability to achieve its objectives.	Media coverage, government policies, and local communities can significantly influence companies like Tata Motors.

Macroenvironment

Unlike the microenvironment, the **macroenvironment** includes external, larger societal factors that a business has no control over. These factors often shape the overall business landscape and create both opportunities and threats for businesses.

Macroenvironment Component	Description	Indian Industry Example
Economic Environment	Factors related to consumer income, purchasing power, inflation, unemployment, and overall economic growth.	During the 2020 pandemic, India's economy faced challenges. Companies like Bajaj Auto adapted by offering more affordable vehicles.
Technological Environment	The pace of technological advancements, innovation, and digital transformation.	India's push for digital payments, led by companies like Paytm, revolutionized the payment system, especially after demonetization.
Political and Legal Environment	Government regulations, political stability, and laws that affect business operations.	The introduction of the GST in India changed the way businesses manage taxes and supply chains.
Cultural Environment	The social values, traditions, and behaviors that shape consumer demand and behavior.	Indian consumers increasingly prefer sustainable and eco-friendly products, influencing brands like Dabur to focus on natural ingredients.
Demographic Environment	Population characteristics such as age, gender, family size, income, education level, and occupation.	With India's young population, companies like Urban Clap cater to millennials looking for home services via easy-to-use apps.
Natural Environment	Factors related to natural resources, environmental sustainability, and climate change.	Unreliable monsoons impact agriculture-dependent businesses, leading companies to invest in sustainable practices like drip irrigation.

Key Forces in the Macroenvironment

1. **Demographics**: Demographic shifts, such as age distribution, population growth, and migration, can reshape a market's demand. In India, the growing middle class and young population have spurred the demand for mobile phones, as seen in the success of Samsung.
2. **Cultural Shifts**: Culture influences customer preferences. For example, India has seen a significant shift towards healthy eating, with brands like Patanjali rising in popularity for offering Ayurvedic, organic products that align with traditional Indian values.
3. **Economic Environment**: Fluctuations in income levels, inflation, and economic cycles heavily influence purchasing power. During the economic slowdown in India in 2019-2020, businesses adjusted their production of low-cost products to suit the market's reduced purchasing power.
4. **Technological Environment**: Advancements in technology are a key driver of change. India's telecom sector, led by Reliance Jio's introduction of affordable 4G services, transformed the entire telecom industry, forcing competitors to innovate rapidly or lose market share.

5. **Political and Legal Factors**: Government policies can significantly affect businesses. The Indian government's decision to ban single-use plastics forced FMCG to find alternatives for product packaging.
6. **Natural Environment**: The increasing impact of climate change is forcing industries to rethink their strategies. Agriculture-dependent businesses in India have begun investing in weather-resistant crops and irrigation technology to counter unpredictable monsoons.

The Importance of Environmental Scanning

Environmental scanning is the process of monitoring and analyzing the marketing environment to identify trends, threats, and opportunities. Businesses in India, like Flipkart actively use environmental scanning to:

1. **Predict Market Trends**: Identifying emerging trends allows businesses to develop proactive strategies rather than reactive measures.
2. **Understand Competitive Dynamics**: By scanning the microenvironment, companies can predict competitor actions and adjust their own strategies to maintain a competitive edge.
3. **Identify Potential Threats**: Monitoring external factors helps businesses mitigate risks such as political instability, economic downturns, or supply chain disruptions.
4. **Discover New Opportunities**: Environmental scanning often reveals untapped markets or growing trends. For instance, the surge in smartphone usage in India opened up significant opportunities for mobile app like Zomato.

Strategic Implications for Businesses in India

For businesses to survive and thrive in the dynamic Indian market, they must embrace strategies that take the marketing environment into account. Some critical strategies businesses should adopt:

1. **Adapt to Technological Changes**: Companies must invest in technology to remain competitive. For example, India's leading education technology company, Byju's, took advantage of the digital education trend to create a robust e-learning platform during the pandemic.
2. **Leverage Demographic Shifts**: Understanding demographic trends is crucial. For instance, Ola Cabs understood the growing need for ride-hailing services in urban areas and introduced affordable transportation solutions like auto-rickshaws in its app.
3. **Stay Culturally Relevant**: Companies must align with the cultural values of their target audience. Titan watches, for example, successfully captured the Indian market by creating culturally relevant advertisements during festive seasons like Diwali.
4. **Compliance with Legal Regulations**: To avoid legal troubles, companies must always remain compliant with local laws. After the introduction of the Consumer Protection Act, Indian e-commerce platforms revised their return policies to meet legal standards.
5. **Sustainability and the Natural Environment**: As India becomes more environmentally conscious, businesses must adopt eco-friendly practices. Tata Chemicals, for instance, has implemented sustainable practices in water management and reduced emissions to align with environmental regulations.

Understanding the marketing environment is critical to the long-term success of any business. Like Ramesh, who learned to adapt to changing weather patterns and new competitors, businesses must constantly monitor both their micro and macro environments. This understanding allows businesses to proactively plan for changes, minimize risks, and capitalize on opportunities.

In a country as dynamic and diverse as India, the marketing environment is continually evolving. Businesses that stay ahead of these changes are the ones that will thrive, while those that ignore these forces risk falling behind.

CHAPTER III

The Enigma of Consumer Behavior

The Puzzle of the Bazaar

In the heart of Mumbai, amidst the bustling streets and vibrant markets, there lived a shopkeeper named Raj. Raj had inherited his family's small shop, a humble establishment that sold a variety of goods, from spices to fabrics. Despite the shop's prime location, Raj struggled to understand why some customers walked in, browsed, and left without buying anything, while others seemed eager to make a purchase the moment they stepped inside.

One evening, after another day of puzzling over his customers' behavior, Raj sat down with his grandfather, a wise old man who had run the shop for decades. "Why do some customers buy and others don't?" Raj asked, perplexed.

His grandfather smiled and handed him an old notebook. "This," he said, "is the key to understanding the mystery of our customers. It's all about knowing what drives them—their desires, fears, habits, and motivations. You see, selling isn't just about having the right products; it's about understanding the minds of those who walk through our doors."

Intrigued, Raj opened the notebook and began to delve into the world of consumer behavior, a journey that would soon unlock the secrets of the bazaar.

2.1 What is Consumer Behavior?

Raj's First Lesson:

As Raj began to read, he learned that **consumer behavior** is the study of how individuals, groups, or organizations select, buy, use, and dispose of goods, services, ideas, or experiences to satisfy their needs and desires. This behavior is influenced by a complex interplay of factors, ranging from personal and psychological to social and cultural.

Meaning of Consumer Behavior:

Consumer behavior refers to the actions and decision-making processes of buyers when they purchase goods and services. It encompasses everything from the initial recognition of a need or desire to the final purchase decision and post-purchase evaluation.

Famous Definitions of Consumer Behavior:

1. **Philip Kotler:***"Consumer behavior is the study of how individuals, groups, and organizations select, buy, use, and dispose of goods, services, ideas, or experiences to satisfy their needs and desires."*

Significance: Kotler's definition emphasizes the broad scope of consumer behavior, including the entire process from selecting to disposing of products.

1. **Loudon and Della Bitta:***"Consumer behavior is the decision process and physical activity individuals engage in when evaluating, acquiring, using, or disposing of goods and services."*

Significance: This definition highlights the active role of consumers in evaluating and using products, not just the purchasing aspect.

3. **Schiffman and Kanuk:***"Consumer behavior is the behavior that consumers display in searching for, purchasing, using, evaluating, and disposing of products and services that they expect will satisfy their needs."*

Significance: Schiffman and Kanuk focus on the expectations and satisfaction of needs, which are central to understanding why consumers make certain decisions.

Importance of Understanding Consumer Behavior:

Understanding consumer behavior is crucial for businesses because it helps them to create products and services that meet the needs of their customers more effectively. By understanding what drives consumers' choices, businesses can tailor their marketing strategies to attract and retain customers, improve customer satisfaction, and ultimately drive sales.

1. **Product Development and Innovation:**
    - Consumer behavior insights guide the development of new products or the improvement of existing ones by identifying what consumers value.
    - **Example:** Raj learned that many of his customers preferred organic spices, leading him to introduce a new line of organic products.
2. **Effective Marketing Strategies:**
    - By understanding consumer behavior, businesses can design marketing campaigns that resonate with their target audience.
    - **Example:** Raj noticed that his customers responded well to discounts during festivals, so he planned special promotions around these times.
3. **Improving Customer Experience:**
    - Understanding consumer behavior helps businesses enhance the customer experience by addressing pain points and exceeding expectations.
    - **Example:** Raj realized that customers often left without buying because they couldn't find what they were looking for, so he reorganized his shop to make products more accessible.
4. **Predicting Market Trends:**
    - Consumer behavior research can help predict future trends, enabling businesses to stay ahead of the competition.
    - **Example:** Raj noticed a growing interest in eco-friendly products, prompting him to stock more sustainable items.

2.2 Determinants of Consumer Behavior

As Raj read further, he discovered that consumer behavior is shaped by a variety of determinants. These factors influence the decisions consumers make, from choosing a product to the brand they prefer.

1. Cultural Factors

Culture plays a significant role in shaping consumer behavior. It includes the values, beliefs, customs, and rituals that are shared by a group of people. These cultural elements influence how consumers perceive products and brands, what they value, and how they make purchasing decisions.

- **Example:** In India, cultural values such as family, tradition, and spirituality influence consumer behavior significantly. For instance, during festivals like Diwali, there is a strong cultural inclination towards buying gifts, sweets, and new clothes. Businesses often tailor their marketing strategies around these cultural events to tap into the increased consumer spending.

2. Social Factors

Social factors include influences from family, friends, and social networks. These factors affect consumers' attitudes, beliefs, and behaviors. Social groups, reference groups, and family roles all play a part in shaping consumer choices.

- **Example:** In many Indian households, purchasing decisions, especially for big-ticket items like electronics or cars, are often made collectively by the family. The opinions of family members can heavily influence the final decision, with elders typically having a strong say in what is bought.

3. Personal Factors

Personal factors are characteristics specific to an individual, such as age, gender, occupation, income level, and lifestyle. These factors influence what products consumers buy, how they perceive brands, and how they respond to marketing messages.

- **Example:** A young professional in a metro city like Bengaluru might prefer to spend on convenience products and experiences, such as fast food, online subscriptions, or smart gadgets, that suit their fast-paced lifestyle. In contrast, a retired individual might prioritize health-related products and traditional brands they have trusted for years.

4. Psychological Factors

Psychological factors include a consumer's motivations, perceptions, attitudes, beliefs, and learning. These factors influence how consumers interpret information and make decisions.

- **Motivation:** Motivation refers to the internal drives that push an individual to take action. It is often driven by the desire to satisfy a specific need.

Example: A consumer may be motivated to buy a gym membership due to the desire to improve their health and fitness.

- **Perception:** Perception is how consumers interpret information and form a view of the world. It can be influenced by marketing, personal experiences, and social interactions.

Example: A luxury brand like Louis Vuitton is often perceived as a status symbol, influencing consumers to purchase its products to reflect a certain social standing.

- **Attitudes and Beliefs:** Attitudes are a consumer's consistent evaluations, feelings, and tendencies toward an object or idea. Beliefs are the specific convictions that a person holds as true.

Example: A consumer who believes in environmental sustainability may prefer to buy products from brands that are eco-friendly.

5. Economic Factors

Economic factors such as income, savings, and economic conditions influence consumers' buying behavior. Consumers' purchasing power and the overall economic environment can affect their spending patterns.

- **Example:** During an economic downturn, consumers might reduce their spending on luxury items and focus more on essential goods. Conversely, during times of economic prosperity, there is often an increase in spending on non-essential and luxury goods.

6. Situational Factors

Situational factors are the specific conditions in which consumers make purchasing decisions. These include physical surroundings, social surroundings, time factors, and the consumer's mood or condition at the time of purchase.

- **Example:** A consumer may be more likely to purchase a product in a well-lit, aesthetically pleasing store environment compared to a cluttered or poorly lit space. Similarly, a limited-time discount or a flash sale can create urgency, pushing consumers to make quicker purchasing decisions.

7. Technological Factors

With the rise of digital technology, consumers now have access to more information and can compare products and prices easily. Technology also influences how consumers interact with brands and make purchasing decisions.

- **Example:** The widespread use of smartphones and e-commerce platforms in India has made online shopping a popular choice, especially during sales events like Flipkart's Big Billion Days or Amazon's Great Indian Festival. Consumers are influenced by reviews, ratings, and the convenience of shopping from their phones.

8. Legal and Ethical Factors

Legal and ethical considerations also play a role in shaping consumer behavior. Consumers are increasingly aware of issues such as environmental sustainability, fair trade, and ethical sourcing, which can influence their purchasing decisions.

- **Example:** Companies that ensure their products are cruelty-free or sourced from sustainable materials may attract environmentally conscious consumers.

2.3 The Consumer Decision-Making Process

Raj realized that understanding the determinants of consumer behavior was just the beginning. To truly master the art of selling, he needed to understand how consumers make their purchasing decisions.

The consumer decision-making process involves several stages:

1. Need Recognition

The decision-making process begins when a consumer recognizes a need or problem. This need can be triggered by internal stimuli (e.g., hunger, thirst) or external stimuli (e.g., advertising, word-of-mouth).

- **Example:** Raj noticed that during the summer, customers often came in looking for cool, refreshing beverages. Recognizing this need, he began to stock more soft drinks and chilled juices.

2. Information Search

Once the need is recognized, the consumer searches for information about the products or services that can fulfill it. This search can be internal (based on previous experiences) or external (involving personal contacts, public sources, or marketing communications).

- **Example:** A customer interested in buying a new smartphone might research online reviews, visit stores to compare models, or ask friends and family for recommendations.

3. Evaluation of Alternatives

After gathering information, the consumer evaluates the different options available. This evaluation is based on various criteria such as price, quality, features, and brand reputation.

- **Example:** A customer considering purchasing a laptop might compare different brands and models, weighing the pros and cons of each based on their needs (e.g., processing power, battery life, brand reliability).

4. Purchase Decision

After evaluating the alternatives, the consumer makes a purchase decision. However, this decision can still be influenced by factors such as promotions, discounts, or even the attitude of the salesperson.

- **Example:** Raj observed that when he offered a discount or bundled items together (e.g., buy two, get one free), customers were more likely to make a purchase on the spot.

5. Post-Purchase Behavior

The consumer's experience after the purchase is crucial. If the product meets or exceeds expectations, the consumer is likely to be satisfied and may become a repeat customer. Conversely, if the product falls short, it may lead to dissatisfaction and negative word-of-mouth.

- **Example:** Raj made it a point to ask customers about their satisfaction with products they had previously purchased. This helped him to understand what items were popular and which ones needed improvement or replacement.

2.4 Practical Activity: Analyzing Consumer Behavior

Activity Name: The Customer's Journey

Setup: Divide students into groups and assign each group a different product category (e.g., electronics, clothing, groceries). Each group will identify the factors influencing consumer behavior in their assigned category, from cultural and social factors to psychological and economic ones.

Task: Each group will map out a typical customer's decision-making process for their product category, including the stages of need recognition, information search, evaluation of alternatives, purchase decision, and post-purchase behavior.

Presentation: Groups will present their findings to the class, explaining how different determinants influence consumer behavior in their assigned product category. They should also discuss how businesses can use this understanding to improve their marketing strategies.

Discussion: The class will discuss how these insights can be applied in real-world scenarios, drawing parallels with familiar brands and products.

2.5 Unlocking the Consumer Mind

As Raj closed the notebook, he realized that understanding consumer behavior was like solving a complex puzzle. Every decision a customer makes is influenced by a myriad of factors, each piece fitting together to form a bigger picture. By understanding these determinants—cultural, social, personal, psychological, economic, situational, technological, legal, and ethical—Raj could better anticipate his customers' needs and tailor his offerings to meet them.

The key to success, Raj learned, wasn't just in having the right products but in understanding the minds of those who would buy them. With this newfound knowledge, he felt ready to unlock the full potential of his shop, transforming it from a small, struggling business into a thriving, customer-centric marketplace.

CHAPTER IV

Crafting the Perfect Fit Market Segmentation, Target Marketing, Differentiation, and Positioning

The Tailor's Secret

In the vibrant city of Jaipur, known for its rich cultural heritage and bustling markets, lived a skilled tailor named Arjun. Arjun was famous for his ability to craft perfect outfits that fit each of his customers like a glove. No matter how unique the customer's shape, size, or preference, Arjun had a knack for creating something that not only looked good but felt just right.

One day, a young entrepreneur named Priya walked into Arjun's shop. She had recently started her own clothing line but was struggling to gain a foothold in the competitive market. Priya admired Arjun's work and asked him, "What's your secret? How do you make each piece of clothing fit so perfectly?"

Arjun smiled and said, "The secret lies in understanding my customers. I don't just make clothes; I create something that fits the person wearing it, both physically and emotionally. Every stitch, every fabric choice, is made with the individual in mind."

Inspired by Arjun's wisdom, Priya realized that success in business wasn't just about creating a product but about ensuring that it perfectly fits the needs and desires of her target customers. And so began her journey into the world of market segmentation, target marketing, differentiation, and positioning.

3.1 Understanding Market Segmentation

Arjun's First Lesson:

As Priya delved deeper into Arjun's approach, she learned that **market segmentation** is the process of dividing a broad consumer or business market, normally consisting of existing and potential customers, into sub-groups of consumers (known as segments) based on some type of shared characteristics.

Meaning of Market Segmentation:

Market segmentation involves dividing a market into distinct groups of buyers who have different needs, characteristics, or behaviors and who might require separate products or marketing mixes. The goal of segmentation is to identify groups of potential customers who are most likely to respond positively to specific marketing strategies.

Famous Definitions of Market Segmentation:

1. **Philip Kotler:***"Market segmentation is the process of dividing a market into distinct groups of buyers who have different needs, characteristics, or behaviors and who might require separate products or marketing mixes."*
2. **Significance:** Kotler's definition highlights the importance of identifying distinct groups within a market that may require tailored marketing strategies.
3. **Smith (1956):***"Market segmentation involves viewing a heterogeneous market as a number of smaller homogeneous markets in response to differing preferences, attributable to the desires of consumers for more precise satisfaction of their varying wants."*
4. **Significance:** Smith's definition emphasizes the idea of breaking down a broad market into smaller, more manageable segments based on consumer preferences.

5. **Wind and Cardozo (1974):**"*Market segmentation is a process by which a market is divided into distinct, meaningful, and identifiable groups or segments based on the common characteristics or needs of the customers within each group.*"
6. **Significance:** This definition underscores the importance of identifying meaningful and identifiable segments within a market.

Importance of Market Segmentation:

Market segmentation allows businesses to focus their efforts on specific groups of customers, tailoring their products and marketing strategies to meet the unique needs of each segment. This targeted approach is more efficient and effective than trying to appeal to an entire market with a single strategy.

1. **Enhanced Customer Satisfaction:**

    - By addressing the specific needs and preferences of each segment, businesses can create more personalized offerings that lead to higher customer satisfaction.
    - **Example:** Priya realized that her younger customers preferred modern, trendy designs, while older customers valued traditional styles. She segmented her market accordingly and developed distinct product lines for each group.

2. **Better Resource Allocation:**

    - Market segmentation helps businesses allocate their resources more effectively by focusing on the most promising segments, leading to better returns on investment.
    - **Example:** Priya decided to allocate more of her marketing budget to online channels that reached her younger, tech-savvy customers, rather than spending equally across all channels.

3. **Improved Competitive Positioning:**

    - By identifying and targeting specific segments, businesses can differentiate themselves from competitors who may be trying to appeal to a broader audience.
    - **Example:** Priya positioned her brand as a specialist in custom-made ethnic wear for young professionals, setting her apart from mass-market clothing brands.

4. **Increased Market Share:**

    - Targeting underserved or niche segments can help businesses capture a larger share of the market by meeting needs that are not being addressed by competitors.
    - **Example:** Priya discovered a niche market for petite sizes, which were not well-served by other brands. By offering a dedicated line for petite customers, she was able to capture this segment and increase her market share.

Types of Market Segmentation:

1. **Geographic Segmentation:**

- **Definition:** Dividing the market based on geographical boundaries such as countries, states, regions, cities, or neighborhoods.
- **Example:** A company like **Amul** might market different products in various parts of India, such as selling more ghee in northern states and more butter in southern states, based on regional dietary preferences.

2. **Demographic Segmentation:**

    - **Definition:** Dividing the market based on demographic variables such as age, gender, income, education, occupation, and family size.
    - **Example:Horlicks**, a nutritional supplement, targets different demographic segments with specific products like Junior Horlicks for children, Women's Horlicks for women, and Horlicks for senior citizens.

3. **Psychographic Segmentation:**

    - **Definition:** Dividing the market based on lifestyle, social class, personality traits, and values.
    - **Example:Tata Nano** initially targeted lower-income segments looking for affordable car ownership but also tapped into psychographic segments that valued simplicity and practicality over luxury.

4. **Behavioral Segmentation:**

    - **Definition:** Dividing the market based on consumer knowledge, attitudes, uses, or responses to a product.
    - **Example:Nestlé Maggi** uses behavioral segmentation by targeting busy working professionals and students who seek convenience and quick meal solutions.

3.2 Target Marketing: Choosing the Right Audience

Arjun's Second Lesson:

Once Priya understood the importance of segmentation, Arjun explained the next step: **target marketing**. Target marketing involves selecting one or more segments to focus marketing efforts on, choosing the segments that offer the best opportunities for success.

Meaning of Target Marketing:

Target marketing is the process of evaluating each market segment's attractiveness and selecting one or more segments to enter. It's about deciding where to focus your marketing efforts to achieve the best results.

Famous Definitions of Target Marketing:

1. **Philip Kotler:**"*Target marketing is the process of identifying and evaluating various segments of a market and then selecting one or more segments as the focus for the marketing mix.*"
2. **Significance:** Kotler's definition emphasizes the importance of carefully evaluating each segment before selecting the one(s) to target.
3. **Sengupta (2005):**"*Target marketing involves breaking a market into segments and then concentrating marketing efforts on one or a few key segments.*"
4. **Significance:** Sengupta highlights the strategic decision-making involved in choosing which segments to focus on.

Importance of Target Marketing:

Target marketing allows businesses to concentrate their resources on the most promising segments, ensuring that their marketing efforts are more efficient and effective. By focusing on specific segments, businesses can create tailored marketing messages that resonate more strongly with their target audience.

1. **Increased Marketing Efficiency:**

   - By focusing on specific segments, businesses can use their resources more efficiently, avoiding the waste associated with broad, untargeted marketing efforts.
   - **Example:** Priya decided to focus her marketing efforts on young professionals, as this segment showed the most potential for growth and profitability.

2. **Stronger Customer Relationships:**

   - Target marketing allows businesses to develop deeper relationships with their customers by addressing their specific needs and preferences.
   - **Example:** Priya created a loyalty program for her target customers, offering exclusive discounts and early access to new collections, which helped build a loyal customer base.

3. **Competitive Advantage:**

   - By targeting a specific segment, businesses can differentiate themselves from competitors who may be trying to appeal to a broader audience.
   - **Example:** Priya positioned her brand as a go-to destination for stylish, professional attire for young women, setting her apart from competitors who offered more generic clothing options.

Approaches to Target Marketing:

1. **Undifferentiated (Mass) Marketing:**

   - **Definition:** A strategy where the company ignores segment differences and targets the whole market with one offer.
   - **Example:Coca-Cola** originally used undifferentiated marketing, offering the same product to the entire market without variation.

2. **Differentiated (Segmented) Marketing:**

   - **Definition:** A strategy where the company targets several market segments with a different offering for each.
   - **Example:Hindustan Unilever Limited (HUL)** uses differentiated marketing with its range of soaps, offering products like **Lifebuoy** for hygiene-conscious consumers and **Lux** for those seeking beauty-enhancing products.

3. **Concentrated (Niche) Marketing:**

   - **Definition:** A strategy where the company targets a large share of one or a few smaller segments or niches.
   - **Example:Ferrari** focuses on a niche market of luxury sports car enthusiasts, offering highly specialized products for a small, affluent segment.

4. **Micromarketing (Local or Individual Marketing):**

    - **Definition:** A strategy where the company tailors products and marketing programs to suit the tastes of specific individuals or locations.
    - **Example:Big Bazaar** tailors its product offerings to meet the preferences of local customers in different regions of India, sometimes even at the store level.

3.3 Differentiation: Standing Out in the Crowd

Arjun's Third Lesson:

With the target market identified, Arjun emphasized the importance of **differentiation**. Differentiation is about creating a unique product or service that stands out from the competition and provides value to the target market.

Meaning of Differentiation:

Differentiation is the process of distinguishing a product or service from others in the market to make it more attractive to a particular target market. It involves developing a unique value proposition that appeals to the specific needs and desires of the target audience.

Famous Definitions of Differentiation:

1. **Michael Porter:***"Differentiation involves creating something that is perceived industry-wide as being unique. It is one of the two basic types of competitive advantage a firm can possess."*
2. **Significance:** Porter emphasizes that differentiation is a key source of competitive advantage, allowing a firm to stand out in a crowded market.
3. **Philip Kotler:***"Differentiation is the act of designing a set of meaningful differences to distinguish the company's offering from competitors' offerings."*
4. **Significance:** Kotler's definition focuses on the importance of creating meaningful differences that resonate with consumers.

Importance of Differentiation:

Differentiation is crucial because it helps a company to establish a competitive advantage. When a product or service is perceived as unique and valuable, it can attract and retain customers, even in highly competitive markets.

1. **Building Brand Loyalty:**

    - Differentiation creates a unique identity for a brand, which can lead to strong customer loyalty.
    - **Example:** Priya's customers appreciated the personalized service and unique designs offered by her brand, which kept them coming back.

2. **Commanding Premium Prices:**

    - Products or services that are differentiated and perceived as high-quality or unique can command higher prices.
    - **Example:** Priya was able to charge premium prices for her custom-made clothing, as her customers valued the quality and uniqueness of her designs.

3. **Reducing Price Competition:**
    - Differentiation reduces the reliance on price competition, as customers are willing to pay more for a product they perceive as unique.
    - **Example:** Unlike her competitors, Priya didn't have to rely on discounts to attract customers, as they were willing to pay full price for her distinctive products.

Ways to Differentiate:

1. **Product Differentiation:**
    - **Definition:** Differentiating a product based on its features, performance, style, or design.
    - **Example:Apple** differentiates its products through sleek design, advanced technology, and a strong brand image, making its iPhones highly desirable.
2. **Service Differentiation:**
    - **Definition:** Differentiating a company's services by offering superior customer service, convenience, or support.
    - **Example:Amazon** differentiates itself by offering fast, reliable delivery services through Amazon Prime, enhancing the overall customer experience.
3. **Channel Differentiation:**
    - **Definition:** Differentiating based on the way a company distributes its products or services.
    - **Example:Nike** uses both exclusive brand stores and a strong online presence to provide customers with multiple channels to purchase its products.
4. **People Differentiation:**
    - **Definition:** Differentiating based on the quality of a company's employees and the service they provide.
    - **Example:Taj Hotels** differentiates itself by offering personalized, high-quality service that makes guests feel valued and special.
5. **Image Differentiation:**
    - **Definition:** Differentiating based on a brand's image, which can be created through branding, advertising, and public relations.
    - **Example:Ray-Ban** differentiates its sunglasses through a strong brand image associated with style, quality, and timeless fashion.

3.4 Positioning: Creating a Strong Market Perception

Arjun's Final Lesson:

The last piece of the puzzle was **positioning**. Arjun explained that positioning is about creating a specific image or perception of a product in the minds of the target market. It's how a company wants its product to be perceived relative to competitors.

Meaning of Positioning:

Positioning is the process of defining how a product or brand will be perceived in the market, relative to competitors. It involves crafting a clear, distinctive, and desirable place in the minds of the target audience.

Famous Definitions of Positioning:

1. **Al Ries and Jack Trout:***"Positioning is not what you do to a product. Positioning is what you do to the mind of the prospect."*
2. **Significance:** Ries and Trout emphasize that positioning is about influencing the perception of the product in the consumer's mind, rather than just changing the product itself.
3. **Philip Kotler:***"Positioning is the act of designing the company's offering and image to occupy a distinctive place in the mind of the target market."*
4. **Significance:** Kotler's definition highlights the importance of designing both the product offering and the brand image to achieve effective positioning.

Importance of Positioning:

Effective positioning helps a brand to occupy a distinct and valued place in the target audience's mind, making it easier for customers to understand the unique benefits of the product and why it is a better choice than competing options.

1. **Building Brand Equity:**
    - Positioning strengthens a brand's equity by creating a strong, positive association in the minds of consumers.
    - **Example:** Priya positioned her brand as a luxury label for young professionals, which helped build strong brand equity over time.
2. **Differentiating from Competitors:**
    - Positioning sets a brand apart from competitors by emphasizing its unique value proposition.
    - **Example:** Priya's brand was positioned as offering high-quality, custom-designed clothing, differentiating it from fast-fashion competitors.
3. **Guiding Marketing Strategies:**
    - A clear positioning strategy guides all marketing efforts, ensuring consistency in messaging and branding.
    - **Example:** Priya's marketing campaigns consistently highlighted the quality and exclusivity of her designs, reinforcing her brand's positioning.

Steps in Positioning:

1. **Identify Competitors:**
    - Analyze the competitors in the market to understand their positioning and how they are perceived by consumers.
    - **Example:Maruti Suzuki** analyzed competitors like Hyundai and Tata to position its cars as reliable and value-for-money options.

2. **Determine Points of Differentiation (PODs):**
    - Identify the key features or benefits that make the product stand out from competitors.
    - **Example:Parle-G** positioned itself as a nutritious and affordable biscuit, appealing to health-conscious and budget-conscious consumers alike.

3. **Create a Positioning Statement:**
    - Develop a concise statement that clearly communicates the product's unique value to the target market.
    - **Example:Maggi's** positioning statement might be: "The 2-minute noodle that brings joy and convenience to your mealtime."

4. **Communicate the Positioning:**
    - Use marketing channels such as advertising, packaging, and social media to consistently communicate the product's positioning to the target audience.
    - **Example:Fevicol** consistently communicates its positioning as the strongest adhesive through creative and memorable advertisements.

3.5 Practical Activity: Crafting the Perfect Fit

Activity Name: The Positioning Map

- **Setup:** Students will use the target market and product category from previous activities. Each group will create a positioning map, plotting their product and its competitors based on key attributes such as price, quality, and unique features.
- **Task:** Groups will identify where their product currently stands and where they want it to be positioned in the market.
- **Presentation:** Groups will present their positioning maps and positioning statements, explaining how they will achieve their desired position in the market.
- **Discussion:** The class will discuss the challenges of positioning and how a clear positioning strategy can lead to a stronger market presence.

As Priya closed her notebook, she understood that succeeding in business was like crafting a tailored outfit. Just as Arjun created garments that perfectly fit his customers, Priya realized that she needed to craft her marketing strategies to fit her target customers' needs and desires.

By segmenting the market, selecting the right target audience, differentiating her products, and positioning her brand effectively, Priya was ready to carve out her own niche in the competitive world of fashion. She knew that with these tools, she could make her clothing line stand out and resonate deeply with her customers.

CHAPTER V

Unveiling the Market's Secrets The Power of Marketing Research

The Detective's Quest

In the vibrant city of Kolkata, where the streets are filled with the aroma of fresh sweets and the sounds of lively chatter, there lived a young woman named Neha. Known for her sharp mind and curiosity, Neha was the go-to person in her community whenever there was a mystery to solve—be it finding a lost item or uncovering the secrets of a strange occurrence.

One day, her uncle, who owned a chain of famous sweet shops in the city, approached her with a problem that had been troubling him for months. "Neha," he began, "my sales have been dipping, and I can't figure out why. I've tried different promotions, but nothing seems to work. Can you help me get to the bottom of this?"

Excited by the challenge, Neha decided to take on the case. She quickly realized that this wasn't just any puzzle—this was a market mystery that needed unraveling. And so, Neha's journey into the world of ***marketing research*** *began, where she would uncover hidden truths that could turn her uncle's business around.*

4.1 What is Marketing Research?

Neha's Initial Discovery:

As Neha embarked on her investigation, she realized that **marketing research** is much like detective work. It involves systematically gathering, analyzing, and interpreting information to uncover insights about the market, customers, competitors, and the broader business environment. The purpose of marketing research is to help businesses make informed decisions, minimize risks, and capitalize on opportunities.

Meaning of Marketing Research:

Marketing research is the backbone of informed decision-making in business. It involves the careful collection and analysis of data related to consumers' needs, preferences, behaviors, and the overall market environment. Through this process, businesses can understand what drives consumer decisions, how the market is evolving, and where new opportunities might lie.

Famous Definitions of Marketing Research:

1. **Philip Kotler:***"Marketing research is the systematic design, collection, analysis, and reporting of data relevant to a specific marketing situation facing an organization."*
2. **Significance:** This definition by Kotler emphasizes the structured approach to marketing research, highlighting the importance of each step—from design to reporting—in addressing specific business challenges.
3. **American Marketing Association (AMA):***"Marketing research is the function that links the consumer, customer, and public to the marketer through information—information used to identify and define marketing opportunities and problems; generate, refine, and evaluate marketing actions; monitor marketing performance; and improve understanding of marketing as a process."*
4. **Significance:** The AMA's definition underscores the role of marketing research in connecting the business with its customers and the broader market, facilitating better decision-making across various marketing functions.
5. **David Aaker:***"Marketing research is the systematic process of gathering, recording, and analyzing data to guide marketing decisions."*
6. **Significance:** Aaker's definition focuses on the systematic nature of marketing research and its ultimate goal: guiding effective marketing decisions.

Importance of Marketing Research:

Marketing research is crucial for businesses because it serves as the foundation for all marketing decisions. Here's why it's important:

1. **Identifying Opportunities and Threats:**
   - Marketing research helps businesses identify new market opportunities, such as emerging consumer trends, and potential threats from competitors or market changes.
   - **Example:** Neha discovered through her research that health-conscious customers were increasingly avoiding sugary sweets, signaling an opportunity for her uncle to introduce healthier alternatives.

2. **Understanding Consumer Needs and Preferences:**
   - Research provides deep insights into what consumers want, their preferences, and their pain points, enabling businesses to tailor their offerings accordingly.
   - **Example:** By surveying customers, Neha learned that many were seeking low-calorie desserts, which her uncle's shop did not currently offer.

3. **Enhancing Product Development:**
   - Marketing research informs product development by providing data on what features or benefits customers value most.
   - **Example:** Based on her findings, Neha suggested developing a line of sugar-free sweets, a product that aligned with customer preferences and market trends.

4. **Improving Marketing Strategies:**
   - Through research, businesses can refine their marketing strategies, ensuring that their messages resonate with their target audience and that their channels are effective.
   - **Example:** Neha found that her uncle's social media promotions weren't reaching the intended audience, prompting a shift in strategy to more targeted, local advertising.

5. **Reducing Business Risks:**
   - By providing data-driven insights, marketing research reduces the risks associated with launching new products, entering new markets, or making other significant business decisions.
   - **Example:** Before launching the new product line, Neha recommended conducting a small-scale test to gauge customer interest, minimizing the risk of a full-scale launch failure.

Role of Marketing Research:

Marketing research plays several critical roles in a business:

- **Decision-Making Tool:** It provides the information needed to make informed decisions about marketing strategies, product development, pricing, and distribution.

- **Customer Insights:** It helps businesses understand their customers on a deeper level, leading to more effective customer engagement and loyalty.
- **Market Trends:** It identifies emerging market trends that can shape future business strategies.
- **Competitive Advantage:** It offers insights into competitors' strengths and weaknesses, helping businesses position themselves effectively in the market.
- **Innovation Catalyst:** It fosters innovation by revealing unmet needs or new customer preferences that can inspire new products or services.

4.2 Types of Marketing Research

Neha's Deep Dive:

As Neha delved further into her research, she discovered that there are different types of marketing research, each serving a unique purpose in the decision-making process.

1. Primary Research: Gathering Original Insights

Primary research involves collecting new, original data directly from the source. This type of research is customized to address specific business needs and provides firsthand insights.

- **Methods of Primary Research:**

  1. **Surveys:**

     - **Definition:** Surveys involve asking a set of questions to a selected group of people to gather information about their opinions, behaviors, or preferences.
     - **Example:** Neha conducted surveys in the local neighborhood to understand why customers were choosing her uncle's competitors over his shop.
     - **Link to Story:** Neha found that many customers were not aware of the shop's latest offerings, indicating a need for better communication.

  2. **Interviews:**

     - **Definition:** Interviews involve one-on-one discussions with individuals to gain in-depth insights into their thoughts, experiences, and preferences.
     - **Example:** Neha interviewed loyal customers to understand what kept them coming back and what improvements they would like to see.
     - **Link to Story:** Through these interviews, Neha discovered that customers appreciated the traditional recipes but wanted to see more innovative options.

  3. **Focus Groups:**

     - **Definition:** Focus groups involve guided discussions with a small group of people to gather diverse opinions on a product, service, or idea.
     - **Example:** Neha organized a focus group with local residents to get feedback on potential new products before launching them.
     - **Link to Story:** The focus group provided valuable feedback, helping Neha fine-tune the new product line to better meet customer expectations.

4. **Observations:**

    - **Definition:** Observational research involves watching how consumers interact with products or services in a natural setting.
    - **Example:** Neha spent hours observing customers in the shop, noting which products they were drawn to and how they made their purchasing decisions.
    - **Link to Story:** Neha noticed that customers often hesitated at the health section, suggesting a need for clearer signage and better product placement.

2. Secondary Research: Leveraging Existing Data

Secondary research involves analyzing data that has already been collected by others. This type of research can provide valuable background information and context for primary research findings.

- **Sources of Secondary Research:**

1. **Industry Reports:**

    - **Definition:** Reports published by industry organizations or research firms that provide insights into market trends, consumer behavior, and competitive dynamics.
    - **Example:** Neha reviewed industry reports on confectionery trends to understand broader market dynamics and consumer preferences.
    - **Link to Story:** These reports confirmed the growing demand for health-conscious products, reinforcing Neha's strategy to introduce sugar-free sweets.

2. **Government Publications:**

    - **Definition:** Data and reports published by government agencies on demographics, economic indicators, and consumer spending patterns.
    - **Example:** Neha used government data on local demographics to better understand the income levels and purchasing power in her uncle's shop's vicinity.
    - **Link to Story:** This data helped Neha tailor the shop's product offerings to better align with the economic profile of the area.

3. **Academic Journals:**

    - **Definition:** Research papers and articles written by scholars that provide theoretical insights and detailed analyses of consumer behavior and marketing strategies.
    - **Example:** Neha referred to academic journals on consumer psychology to understand the factors influencing sweet consumption.
    - **Link to Story:** The journals provided insights into the psychological triggers that could be used in the shop's marketing materials.

4. **Competitor Analysis:**

    - **Definition:** The process of studying competitors' strategies, strengths, weaknesses, and market positions.

- **Example:** Neha analyzed the marketing tactics of the new competitor to identify what made their products more appealing.
- **Link to Story:** By understanding the competitor's strengths, Neha could develop strategies to differentiate her uncle's shop and regain lost customers.

4.3 New Concepts in Marketing Research

Neha's Epiphany:

As Neha continued her research, she realized that modern marketing research has evolved significantly, incorporating new tools and methodologies that make the process more efficient, accurate, and insightful. These new concepts have revolutionized how businesses gather and use information to make decisions.

1. Data-Driven Decision Making:

- **Definition:** Modern marketing research is increasingly data-driven, leveraging big data analytics, artificial intelligence (AI), and machine learning to gain deeper insights into consumer behavior, market trends, and competitive landscapes.
- **Importance:** This approach allows businesses to make more informed decisions based on large volumes of data, identifying patterns and trends that would be impossible to detect manually.
- **Example:** Neha used AI tools to analyze customer feedback from social media, uncovering trends and sentiments that guided the shop's product development and marketing strategies.

2. Real-Time Analytics:

- **Definition:** The speed of information flow has increased, making real-time data collection and analysis crucial. Businesses now have the tools to monitor consumer behavior and market changes in real-time, allowing for more agile decision-making.
- **Importance:** Real-time analytics enable businesses to respond quickly to changes in the market, such as shifts in consumer preferences or emerging trends.
- **Example:** Neha implemented a system that tracked real-time sales data across her uncle's shops, allowing her to adjust promotions and inventory on the fly.

3. Customer-Centricity:

- **Definition:** There's a stronger emphasis on understanding the customer journey holistically. This includes not just their purchasing behaviors, but also their emotions, experiences, and interactions across various touchpoints.
- **Importance:** A customer-centric approach ensures that businesses are focused on creating value for their customers at every stage of their journey, leading to higher satisfaction and loyalty.
- **Example:** Neha mapped out the customer journey from the moment they entered the shop to after-sales interactions, identifying key touchpoints where improvements could enhance the overall experience.

4. Integration of Qualitative and Quantitative Data:

- **Definition:** Modern marketing research integrates qualitative insights (e.g., customer emotions, brand perceptions) with quantitative data (e.g., sales figures, survey ratings) to provide a more complete picture of the market.
- **Importance:** By combining these two types of data, businesses can gain a deeper understanding of their customers and make more informed decisions.

- **Example:** Neha combined quantitative data from sales reports with qualitative insights from customer interviews, leading to a more nuanced understanding of customer preferences.

5. Ethical Considerations and Consumer Privacy:

- **Definition:** With growing concerns about data privacy and ethical marketing practices, modern marketing research must adhere to strict guidelines to protect consumer information and ensure that research practices are ethical and transparent.
- **Importance:** Ethical research practices build trust with consumers and protect the business from legal issues related to data privacy.
- **Example:** Neha ensured that all customer data collected during her research was anonymized and stored securely, in compliance with data protection regulations.

6. Globalization and Cultural Sensitivity:

- **Definition:** As businesses operate in more diverse, global markets, marketing research has to be culturally sensitive and adaptable to different regions, reflecting the varied needs and preferences of global consumers.
- **Importance:** Cultural sensitivity in marketing research ensures that businesses can effectively enter and compete in global markets.
- **Example:** Neha considered the cultural preferences of different neighbourhoods in Kolkata when developing marketing strategies for her uncle's shops, ensuring that each shop's offerings were tailored to local tastes.

7. Sustainability and Social Responsibility:

- **Definition:** Consumers are increasingly valuing brands that demonstrate sustainability and social responsibility. Marketing research now includes assessing consumer attitudes towards environmental and ethical practices and their impact on brand loyalty.
- **Importance:** Brands that prioritize sustainability and social responsibility are more likely to attract and retain customers who are concerned about environmental and social issues.
- **Example:** Neha researched customer attitudes towards sustainability and found that offering eco-friendly packaging for sweets could enhance the shop's appeal to environmentally conscious customers.

4.4 New Definition of Marketing Research

Considering these new concepts, the definition of marketing research has evolved to encompass the modern tools, methodologies, and ethical considerations that define its current and future state:

"Marketing research is the systematic, data-driven process of gathering, analyzing, and interpreting information about consumers, competitors, and the market environment to guide strategic decision-making. It integrates real-time analytics with qualitative and quantitative data to provide holistic insights into consumer behaviors and preferences, ensuring that business strategies are customer-centric, culturally sensitive, and ethically sound. This process not only identifies market opportunities and threats but also supports sustainable and socially responsible business practices in a globalized market."

Key Aspects of This New Definition:

1. **Systematic and Data-Driven:** Emphasizes the structured approach to research while integrating modern data analytics tools and methodologies.
2. **Holistic Insights:** Combines qualitative and quantitative data to offer a comprehensive view of the market and consumer behavior.

3. **Real-Time Analytics:** Reflects the importance of agility and real-time data in making timely and effective business decisions.
4. **Customer-Centricity:** Ensures that all research efforts are focused on understanding and meeting the needs of the consumer.
5. **Cultural Sensitivity and Global Perspective:** Acknowledges the importance of cultural understanding in today's global market.
6. **Ethical Practices:** Highlights the necessity of ethical considerations, particularly in data privacy and consumer protection.
7. **Sustainability and Social Responsibility:** Recognizes the growing importance of assessing and incorporating sustainable and ethical practices in business strategies.

4.5 The Marketing Research Process

Neha's Methodical Approach:

Neha realized that to conduct effective marketing research, she needed to follow a structured process. She learned that the **marketing research process** consists of several key steps:

1. Define the Problem and Research Objectives

The first step is to clearly define the problem that needs to be addressed and establish the research objectives. This involves understanding what information is needed and why it is important.

- **Example:** Neha defined the problem as the declining sales in her uncle's shops and set the research objective to identify the reasons for this decline and potential solutions.

2. Develop the Research Plan

The next step is to develop a detailed research plan, outlining the research methods, sampling techniques, and data collection processes that will be used to gather the necessary information.

- **Example:** Neha developed a research plan that included conducting customer surveys, competitor analysis, and observational research in the shops.

3. Collect the Data

Data collection is the most critical phase of marketing research. It involves gathering the required information using the methods outlined in the research plan.

- **Example:** Neha and her team distributed surveys to customers, interviewed key stakeholders, and observed customer behavior in the shops.

4. Analyze the Data

Once the data is collected, it must be analyzed to uncover patterns, trends, and insights that can help address the research objectives.

- **Example:** Neha analyzed the survey responses and observational data to identify common themes and factors contributing to the decline in sales.

5. Present the Findings

The research findings need to be organized and presented in a clear and actionable format. This usually involves creating reports, charts, and presentations that summarize the key insights and recommendations.

- **Example:** Neha prepared a report for her uncle, highlighting the key findings from the research and suggesting strategies to improve sales, such as introducing healthier product options and enhancing customer service.

6. Make Decisions and Take Action

The final step is to use the research findings to make informed decisions and implement the recommended actions to address the problem.

- **Example:** Based on Neha's recommendations, her uncle introduced new product lines and launched targeted promotions, leading to a gradual recovery in sales.

Practical Activity: The Research Project*Activity Name: Solving the Mystery*

- **Setup:** Students will be assigned a mock business scenario with a specific marketing problem to solve (e.g., declining sales, low customer engagement, poor product performance).
- **Task:** Each group will follow the marketing research process to define the problem, develop a research plan, collect data (using mock data or case studies), analyze the findings, and present their recommendations.
- **Presentation:** Groups will present their research findings and recommendations to the class, simulating a real-world business presentation.
- **Discussion:** The class will discuss the challenges of conducting marketing research and the importance of each step in making data-driven decisions.

Solving the Marketing Mystery

As Neha wrapped up her research project, she realized that marketing research was like being a detective, uncovering the hidden truths that could make or break a business. By systematically gathering and analyzing data, she was able to provide her uncle with actionable insights that helped him turn around his business.

Neha knew that marketing research wasn't just about collecting data; it was about understanding the market, identifying opportunities, and making informed decisions. With the knowledge she had gained, Neha felt ready to tackle any business challenge that came her way.

CHAPTER VI

The Backbone of Strategic Decisions Marketing Information System

The CEO's Dilemma

In the bustling city of Bengaluru, known for its thriving tech industry, there was a company named FusionTech, a mid-sized enterprise that produced innovative consumer electronics. The CEO, Rohan, was a visionary leader who had taken the company to new heights over the past decade. However, as the company grew, Rohan faced a new challenge—making informed decisions in an increasingly complex and competitive market.

One day, during a critical board meeting, Rohan was presented with conflicting reports about the company's performance in different regions. The sales team reported declining numbers in the North, while marketing claimed that brand awareness was at an all-time high. Rohan was confused and frustrated. How could he make the right decisions when the information was inconsistent and scattered across different departments?

After the meeting, Rohan met with his old mentor, Ravi, a retired business strategist who had successfully navigated similar challenges in his career. "Ravi," Rohan said, "I'm overwhelmed. I have data coming in from all sides, but it's disorganized, and I can't see the bigger picture. How can I make the right decisions for my company?"

Ravi smiled and said, "Rohan, what you need is a Marketing Information System. It's like the nervous system of your business—connecting all the different parts and giving you a clear view of what's happening. With an MIS, you'll have the right information at your fingertips to make informed decisions."

Intrigued, Rohan decided to implement a Marketing Information System at FusionTech, a decision that would revolutionize how the company operated.

5.1 What is a Marketing Information System (MIS)?

Rohan's First Step:

As Rohan began to learn about the concept, he understood that a **Marketing Information System (MIS)** is a comprehensive system that gathers, processes, stores, and disseminates information to support marketing decision-making within an organization. Just like Ravi had explained, the MIS serves as the nervous system of the company, ensuring that all relevant data flows seamlessly to where it's needed.

Meaning of Marketing Information System (MIS):

A Marketing Information System (MIS) is a structured arrangement of data, systems, tools, and processes that gather, store, analyze, and distribute timely and relevant information to marketing decision-makers. It ensures that the right information reaches the right people at the right time, enabling them to make informed marketing decisions.

Famous Definitions of Marketing Information System:

1. **Philip Kotler:**"*A Marketing Information System is a system that consists of people, equipment, and procedures to gather, sort, analyze, evaluate, and distribute needed, timely, and accurate information to marketing decision-makers.*"
2. **Significance:** Kotler's definition emphasizes the role of MIS in ensuring that decision-makers have access to timely and accurate information.
3. **William Stanton:**"*A Marketing Information System is an interacting, continuing, future-oriented structure of people, equipment, and procedures designed to generate and process an information flow to aid managerial decision-making in a company's marketing program.*"
4. **Significance:** Stanton highlights the continuous and interactive nature of an MIS, which supports ongoing decision-making.
5. **Peter D. Bennett:**"*A Marketing Information System is a set of procedures and methods for the regular, planned collection, analysis, and presentation of information for use in making marketing decisions.*"

6. **Significance:** Bennett's definition focuses on the systematic approach to collecting and analyzing information within an MIS.

Importance of a Marketing Information System:

Implementing an MIS is crucial for businesses as it acts as the backbone of marketing decision-making. Here's why it's important:

1. **Enhancing Decision-Making:**
    - An MIS provides accurate and up-to-date information that enables marketers to make well-informed decisions.
    - **Example:** At FusionTech, the MIS integrated sales data, market research, and competitor analysis, allowing Rohan to see the full picture and make strategic decisions about where to allocate resources.
2. **Improving Efficiency:**
    - By automating data collection and analysis, an MIS reduces the time and effort required to gather information, allowing businesses to respond quickly to market changes.
    - **Example:** Rohan found that his MIS could generate real-time reports, giving him instant insights into how new product lines were performing across different regions.
3. **Identifying Market Opportunities:**
    - An MIS helps businesses identify emerging trends and market opportunities by analyzing consumer behavior and market data.
    - **Example:** The MIS at FusionTech revealed a growing demand for eco-friendly electronics, prompting Rohan to develop a new product line that quickly captured market share.
4. **Supporting Marketing Strategy Development:**
    - An MIS provides the data needed to develop and refine marketing strategies, ensuring that they are based on accurate insights.
    - **Example:** Using the MIS, Rohan's team was able to segment the market more effectively and create targeted campaigns that resonated with different customer groups.
5. **Monitoring and Controlling Marketing Activities:**
    - An MIS allows businesses to track the effectiveness of their marketing activities and make adjustments as needed to achieve their goals.
    - **Example:** FusionTech's MIS tracked the performance of various marketing campaigns, helping Rohan's team to optimize their efforts and maximize ROI.

5.2 Components of a Marketing Information System

As Rohan delved deeper into the workings of an MIS, he discovered that it comprises several key components. Each of these components plays a vital role in ensuring that the system functions effectively and provides the necessary support for decision-making.

1. Internal Records:

Internal records refer to the data that is collected from within the organization. This includes sales data, inventory levels, financial records, and customer databases. Internal records provide valuable insights into a company's operations and performance.

- **Example:** FusionTech's MIS collected data from various departments, such as sales, finance, and customer service, consolidating it into a single system that provided a comprehensive view of the company's performance.

2. Marketing Intelligence:

Marketing intelligence involves gathering information from external sources to understand the broader market environment. This includes monitoring competitors, tracking industry trends, and gathering data on consumer behavior.

- **Example:** FusionTech's MIS integrated external market data, such as competitor product launches and industry reports, allowing Rohan to stay ahead of market trends and respond proactively.

3. Marketing Research:

Marketing research is a systematic process of collecting, analyzing, and interpreting data about a specific market problem or opportunity. It often involves conducting surveys, interviews, focus groups, and other research methods to gather detailed insights.

- **Example:** Before launching a new product, Rohan's team used the MIS to conduct market research that provided valuable insights into consumer preferences and potential demand.

4. Analytical Tools:

Analytical tools are software applications and algorithms that help businesses analyze data and extract meaningful insights. These tools can include statistical analysis software, data visualization tools, and predictive modeling software.

- **Example:** FusionTech's MIS included advanced analytical tools that allowed Rohan's team to create visual reports and dashboards, making it easier to interpret sales trends and customer behavior.

5. Marketing Decision Support System (MDSS):

A Marketing Decision Support System (MDSS) is a specialized component of an MIS that provides interactive tools for decision-making. It helps marketers explore different scenarios, evaluate options, and make decisions based on data-driven insights.

- **Example:** FusionTech's MDSS enabled Rohan to simulate various pricing strategies for new products, helping him to determine the most effective pricing model to maximize profitability.

5.3 Functions of a Marketing Information System

Rohan realized that the effectiveness of an MIS depends on how well it performs its key functions. These functions ensure that the right information is collected, processed, and delivered to decision-makers in a timely manner.

1. Data Collection:

The first function of an MIS is to collect relevant data from both internal and external sources. This data forms the foundation for all subsequent analysis and decision-making.

- **Example:** FusionTech's MIS collected data from a wide range of sources, including sales records, customer feedback, social media analytics, and market research studies.

2. Data Storage:

Once collected, the data needs to be stored securely and organized in a way that makes it easy to retrieve when needed. Data storage systems can include databases, data warehouses, and cloud storage solutions.

- **Example:** FusionTech's MIS stored all data in a centralized, cloud-based database, ensuring that Rohan and his team could access historical data at any time, from anywhere.

3. Data Processing:

Data processing involves cleaning, organizing, and transforming raw data into a format that can be analyzed. This step is crucial for ensuring that the data is accurate, consistent, and ready for analysis.

- **Example:** The MIS at FusionTech automatically processed incoming data, removing duplicates, correcting errors, and categorizing information for easy analysis.

4. Data Analysis:

The core function of an MIS is to analyze the collected data to extract insights that can inform marketing decisions. This involves using analytical tools to identify patterns, trends, and correlations in the data.

- **Example:** Rohan's team used the MIS to analyze sales trends over the past year, identifying peak seasons, popular products, and potential areas for growth.

5. Information Distribution:

Finally, the MIS distributes the processed information to the relevant decision-makers. This distribution can take the form of reports, dashboards, alerts, or presentations, depending on the needs of the organization.

- **Example:** FusionTech's MIS automatically generated weekly performance reports that were distributed to Rohan and his leadership team, ensuring that everyone had the latest information to make informed decisions.

5.4 The Role of Technology in Marketing Information Systems

As Rohan continued to implement the MIS at FusionTech, he realized that technology plays a critical role in the effectiveness of these systems. Advances in technology have transformed how businesses collect, process, and use marketing information.

1. Big Data and Analytics:

The rise of big data has revolutionized marketing information systems. Big data refers to the vast amounts of structured and unstructured data generated by consumers, businesses, and devices. Advanced analytics tools allow businesses to process and analyze this data to gain deeper insights into consumer behavior and market trends.

- **Example:** FusionTech's MIS integrated big data analytics to track consumer behavior across multiple channels, such as online purchases, social media interactions, and in-store visits. This allowed Rohan's team to gain a comprehensive understanding of their customers.

2. Artificial Intelligence and Machine Learning:

Artificial intelligence (AI) and machine learning (ML) are transforming the capabilities of marketing information systems. These technologies enable the MIS to analyze data more efficiently, identify patterns, and even predict future trends.

- **Example:** FusionTech's MIS used AI to predict which products were likely to be popular in the upcoming season, allowing Rohan to adjust inventory and marketing strategies accordingly.

3. Cloud Computing:

Cloud computing has made it easier for businesses to store and access large amounts of data without the need for expensive on-premises infrastructure. Cloud-based MIS solutions offer scalability, flexibility, and remote access.

- **Example:** FusionTech's MIS was hosted on the cloud, enabling Rohan and his team to access real-time data and reports from anywhere, facilitating remote collaboration and decision-making.

4. Data Visualization Tools:

Data visualization tools help transform complex data into easily understandable charts, graphs, and dashboards. These tools make it easier for decision-makers to interpret data and gain insights quickly.

- **Example:** Rohan used data visualization tools within the MIS to create interactive dashboards that displayed key performance indicators (KPIs) in a visually engaging way, helping him make quick decisions during meetings.

5. Internet of Things (IoT):

The Internet of Things (IoT) connects physical devices to the internet, enabling them to collect and exchange data. In the context of MIS, IoT can provide real-time data from connected devices, such as sensors, smart products, and automated systems.

- **Example:** FusionTech's MIS integrated data from IoT-enabled devices in their manufacturing plants, providing real-time insights into production efficiency and equipment performance.

5.5 Implementing a Marketing Information System

After understanding the components and functions of an MIS, Rohan knew that implementing the system would require careful planning and execution. Here's how he approached the implementation at FusionTech:

1. Needs Assessment:

The first step in implementing an MIS is to assess the specific needs of the organization. This involves identifying the key decisions that need to be supported by the MIS and the types of data required.

- **Example:** Rohan worked with his team to identify the critical areas where they needed better information, such as sales forecasting, customer segmentation, and market trend analysis.

2. System Design:

Once the needs were identified, Rohan's team worked on designing the MIS. This involved selecting the right tools, software, and data sources, as well as defining the processes for data collection, processing, and analysis.

- **Example:** FusionTech's MIS was designed to integrate with existing systems, such as CRM and ERP, ensuring seamless data flow across departments.

3. Data Integration:

Integrating data from various sources is crucial for a successful MIS. This involves connecting internal records, marketing intelligence, and research data into a unified system.

- **Example:** Rohan's team integrated sales data, customer feedback, and competitor analysis into the MIS, providing a comprehensive view of the market.

4. Training and Development:

Implementing an MIS also requires training the team to use the system effectively. This includes educating employees on how to input data, generate reports, and use analytical tools.

- **Example:** FusionTech conducted training sessions for its staff, ensuring that everyone was familiar with the new MIS and could use it to its full potential.

5. Continuous Monitoring and Improvement:

After implementation, it's important to continuously monitor the performance of the MIS and make improvements as needed. This ensures that the system remains effective and aligned with the organization's evolving needs.

- **Example:** Rohan established a feedback loop where employees could suggest improvements to the MIS, ensuring that it continued to meet the company's needs over time.

5.6 Practical Activity: Building Your Own MIS

Activity Name: Designing the Lighthouse

- **Setup:** Divide students into groups and assign each group a fictional company with specific needs (e.g., a retail chain, a tech startup, or a manufacturing company). Each group will design a Marketing Information System tailored to their company's needs.
- **Task:** Groups will identify the key components of their MIS, including data sources, analytical tools, and decision-support features. They will also outline the implementation process, including system design, data integration, and employee training.
- **Presentation:** Groups will present their MIS designs to the class, explaining how their system will support the company's decision-making processes and improve overall efficiency.
- **Discussion:** The class will discuss the challenges of implementing an MIS and how different industries might require different approaches to building and managing such a system.

5.7 Guiding the Business through the Waves

As FusionTech's new Marketing Information System went live, Rohan felt a sense of relief. No longer was he overwhelmed by scattered data and conflicting reports. The MIS provided him with the clarity and insights he needed to make strategic decisions with confidence. Just like the lighthouse guiding a ship through stormy seas, the MIS became the guiding light for FusionTech, ensuring that the company stayed on course, no matter how turbulent the market.

Rohan knew that the success of his business now rested on the shoulders of this powerful system, which connected all parts of the organization and illuminated the path forward. With the MIS in place, FusionTech was not only prepared to weather any storm but also to seize new opportunities as they arose.

CHAPTER VII

Mastering the Art of Product and Product Line Decisions

The Artisan's Workshop

In the ancient city of Varanasi, known for its rich culture and traditional crafts, lived an artisan named Anjali. She was famous for creating exquisite pottery, each piece a work of art in its own right. Her workshop was always filled with customers admiring her creations, but as demand grew, Anjali faced a dilemma.

One day, her apprentice, Rohit, asked, "Master, why don't we expand our product range? We could create a whole line of pottery—dishes, vases, and even sculptures! That way, we can offer something for everyone."

Anjali smiled and said, "Creating new products isn't just about offering more. It's about understanding what fits together, like the pieces of a puzzle. Each product must complement the others, forming a cohesive line that tells a story. This is the art of making product and product line decisions."

Inspired by her wisdom, Rohit began to explore how they could expand their offerings while maintaining the integrity and reputation of their brand. And so, he embarked on a journey to understand the complexities of product and product line decisions.

6.1 What is a Product?

Rohit's First Lesson:

As Rohit learned from Anjali, a **product** is more than just a physical item or service—it's a combination of attributes that provide value to the customer. It includes not only the tangible goods but also the services, brand, and overall experience associated with it.

Meaning of Product:

A product is anything that can be offered to a market to satisfy a want or need. It includes physical goods, services, experiences, events, persons, places, properties, organizations, information, and ideas. Products are at the core of any business's offering and form the basis of customer relationships.

Famous Definitions of Product:

1. **Philip Kotler:***"A product is anything that can be offered to a market for attention, acquisition, use, or consumption that might satisfy a want or need."*
2. **Significance:** Kotler's definition emphasizes the broad nature of products, including not just physical goods but also services, experiences, and ideas.
3. **William J. Stanton:***"A product is a set of tangible and intangible attributes, including packaging, color, price, quality, and brand, plus the seller's services and reputation."*
4. **Significance:** Stanton highlights the combination of tangible and intangible attributes that make up a product, pointing to the importance of brand and reputation.

Core Aspects of a Product:

1. **Core Product:**

    - **Definition:** The core product represents the fundamental benefit or value that the customer is buying.
    - **Example:** For Anjali's pottery, the core product is the aesthetic appeal and utility that the pottery offers.

2. **Actual Product:**
    - **Definition:** The actual product includes the tangible elements, such as features, design, brand name, and packaging.
    - **Example:** Anjali's pottery includes the quality of the clay, the intricate designs, and the brand "Anjali's Artistry."
3. **Expected Product:**
- **Definition:** The set of attributes or characteristics that buyers normally expect and agree to when they purchase a product.
- **Example:** For Anjali's pottery, the expected product includes the durability of the pottery, the vibrant colors, and the smooth finish that customers anticipate.

1. **Augmented Product:**
    - **Definition:** The augmented product consists of additional services and benefits that enhance the product's value.
    - **Example:** Anjali offers personalized customer service and a satisfaction guarantee, which are part of the augmented product.
2. **Potential Product:**
    - **Definition:** All the possible augmentations and transformations the product might undergo in the future. This includes everything that might be done to attract and hold customers.
    - **Example:** For Anjali's pottery, the potential product could include future innovations like smart pottery with embedded sensors, eco-friendly materials, or interactive workshops for customers to create their own designs.

Importance of Understanding Product Decisions:

Understanding product decisions is crucial because these decisions determine the types of products a company will offer, how they will be positioned in the market, and how they will meet the needs of different customer segments.

1. **Meeting Customer Needs:**
    - Product decisions are essential for ensuring that the offerings align with customer preferences and needs.
    - **Example:** Anjali noticed that her customers were increasingly interested in decorative items for their homes. She decided to introduce a new line of artistic vases that catered to this demand.
2. **Building Brand Identity:**
    - The products a company offers define its brand identity. Consistent product decisions help build a strong and recognizable brand.
    - **Example:** Anjali's pottery was known for its intricate designs and quality craftsmanship, which became the hallmark of her brand.
3. **Driving Business Growth:**

- Strategic product decisions, such as introducing new products or expanding product lines, can drive business growth by attracting new customers and increasing sales.
- **Example:** By expanding her product range to include both functional items (like plates) and decorative pieces (like sculptures), Anjali was able to attract a broader audience.

6.2 Types of Products

Rohit soon learned that products can be classified into different categories based on their characteristics and the way they are used by consumers.

1. Consumer Products:

Consumer products are goods and services purchased by individuals for personal use. These products are typically classified into four categories:

1. **Convenience Products:**
   - **Definition:** Products that are purchased frequently, immediately, and with minimal effort.
   - **Example:** Items like soaps, snacks, and basic pottery dishes are convenience products that customers buy regularly.
2. **Shopping Products:**
   - **Definition:** Products that consumers compare based on quality, price, and style before making a purchase decision.
   - **Example:** Customers might compare different designs and prices before choosing an artistic vase or a unique piece of pottery from Anjali's collection.
3. **Specialty Products:**
   - **Definition:** Products with unique characteristics or brand identification that a significant group of buyers is willing to make a special purchase effort to obtain.
   - **Example:** Anjali's custom-made sculptures, which are known for their intricate details and artistic value, are considered specialty products.
4. **Unsought Products:**
   - **Definition:** Products that the consumer does not know about or does not normally think of buying.
   - **Example:** A custom pottery service where Anjali designs personalized pieces for customers is an unsought product until it is introduced and marketed.

2. Industrial Products:

Industrial products are goods used in the production of other goods or services. These products are purchased by businesses rather than individual consumers.

1. **Raw Materials:**
   - **Definition:** Basic materials that are used to produce other goods.
   - **Example:** The clay that Anjali uses to create her pottery is an industrial product purchased from suppliers.

2. **Capital Items:**
    - **Definition:** Products that are used in the production process and have a long life span, such as machinery and equipment.
    - **Example:** The kiln Anjali uses to fire her pottery is a capital item essential for her production process.
3. **Supplies and Services:**
    - **Definition:** Products that are consumed in the production process but do not become part of the final product.
    - **Example:** The paints, glazes, and tools Anjali uses to decorate her pottery fall into this category.

6.3 Product Decisions: The Core of Marketing Strategy

As Rohit's understanding deepened, he realized that product decisions are at the core of a company's marketing strategy. These decisions determine what products will be offered, how they will be differentiated, and how they will be positioned in the market.

1. Product Attributes:

Product attributes refer to the features, quality, and design of a product. These attributes define the product and differentiate it from competitors.

- **Example:** Anjali's pottery is known for its high-quality clay, unique designs, and durable craftsmanship. These attributes make her products stand out in the market.

2. Branding:

Branding involves creating a unique identity for a product through a name, logo, symbol, or design that distinguishes it from competitors.

- **Example:** Anjali branded her pottery under the name "Anjali's Artistry," with a distinctive logo that was imprinted on each piece. This branding helped build recognition and trust among her customers.

3. Packaging:

Packaging is the process of designing and producing the container or wrapper for a product. It plays a crucial role in protecting the product, providing information, and enhancing the product's appeal.

- **Example:** Anjali used eco-friendly packaging for her pottery, which resonated with her environmentally conscious customers. The packaging was also designed to showcase the beauty of the product, making it a key part of the customer experience.

4. Labeling:

Labeling involves creating tags or labels that provide information about the product. Labels can include the brand name, product ingredients, instructions, and other important details.

- **Example:** Each piece of Anjali's pottery came with a label that included the product's name, a brief description of its inspiration, and care instructions, adding to the customer's understanding and appreciation of the product.

5. Product Support Services:

Product support services are additional services that accompany the product, such as customer service, warranties, and after-sales support.

- **Example:** Anjali offered a satisfaction guarantee with all her pottery, promising to replace or repair any piece that was damaged during shipping. This service enhanced customer confidence and loyalty.

6. Product Positioning:

Product positioning refers to how a product is perceived in the minds of consumers relative to competing products. Effective positioning highlights the unique benefits of the product and differentiates it from the competition.

- **Example:** Anjali positioned her pottery as premium, handcrafted art pieces that offered both functional use and decorative appeal. This positioning attracted customers who valued quality and uniqueness.

6.4 Product Line Decisions: Expanding and Managing the Range

Rohit learned that while individual product decisions are important, managing the entire product line is equally crucial for the success of a business. A product line is a group of related products that are marketed under a single brand.

1. Product Line Length:

Product line length refers to the number of items in a product line. Companies must decide whether to expand or contract their product lines based on market demand and strategic goals.

- **Example:** Anjali's original product line included basic pottery items like plates and bowls. As demand grew, she decided to lengthen her product line by adding vases, sculptures, and custom designs.

2. Product Line Depth:

Product line depth refers to the number of variations of each product in the line. This can include different sizes, colors, designs, and quality levels.

- **Example:** Within her line of vases, Anjali offered various sizes, from small bud vases to large floor vases, and different designs, catering to a wide range of customer preferences.

3. Product Line Filling:

Product line filling involves adding more items within the existing range of the product line to take advantage of excess capacity, meet customer needs, or prevent competitors from gaining an advantage.

- **Example:** Anjali noticed a demand for mid-sized vases, which were not currently part of her product line. She decided to fill this gap by introducing a new size, ensuring that her product line catered to all customer needs.

4. Product Line Stretching:

Product line stretching occurs when a company lengthens its product line beyond its current range. This can be done upward, downward, or both.

1. **Downward Stretching:**

    - **Definition:** Introducing lower-end products in the product line to capture a new market segment.

   - **Example:** Anjali introduced a line of more affordable, simpler pottery for customers who admired her work but couldn't afford the high-end pieces.

2. **Upward Stretching:**

   - **Definition:** Introducing higher-end products to target a more affluent market segment.
   - **Example:** To attract upscale customers, Anjali launched a premium line of custom-designed, hand-painted pottery with intricate detailing and luxurious packaging.

3. **Two-Way Stretching:**

   - **Definition:** Extending the product line in both directions, offering both lower-end and higher-end products.
   - **Example:** Anjali decided to stretch her product line both downward and upward, offering both budget-friendly and premium options to capture a wider market.

5. Product Mix Decisions:

Product mix, also known as product assortment, refers to the total variety of products that a company offers. Decisions about the product mix include the width, length, depth, and consistency of the product lines.

- **Example:**

   - **Width:** The variety of product lines offered (e.g., pottery, ceramics, home decor).
   - **Length:** The total number of products within each line (e.g., 10 different types of vases).
   - **Depth:** The number of variations within each product line (e.g., sizes, colors, designs).
   - **Consistency:** How closely related the product lines are in terms of use, production, and distribution (e.g., all of Anjali's products are handcrafted and marketed as luxury items).

6. Product Lifecycle Management:

Product lifecycle management involves managing a product as it goes through its life cycle, from introduction to growth, maturity, and decline. Understanding the product life cycle helps businesses make informed decisions about product development, marketing strategies, and when to introduce new products.

- **Example:** Anjali noticed that interest in her traditional pottery line was declining as more contemporary designs gained popularity. She decided to innovate and introduce a new collection with modern aesthetics while maintaining her brand's quality standards.

6.5 New Product Development and Innovation

As Rohit delved deeper into product strategy, he realized that the creation of new products and the continuous innovation of existing products are critical to maintaining a competitive edge.

1. New Product Development (NPD):

New Product Development is the process of bringing a new product to the market. It involves several stages, from idea generation to commercialization.

- **Stages of NPD:**

1. **Idea Generation:** Gathering ideas from various sources such as customers, competitors, employees, and research.
   - **Example:** Anjali held brainstorming sessions with her team to come up with new product ideas, inspired by customer feedback and market trends.
2. **Idea Screening:** Evaluating ideas to select the most viable ones.
   - **Example:** Anjali screened her ideas to focus on those that aligned with her brand and had the potential to meet market demand.
3. **Concept Development and Testing:** Developing product concepts and testing them with potential customers.
   - **Example:** Anjali created prototypes of new designs and tested them with a select group of loyal customers to gauge their interest.
4. **Business Analysis:** Assessing the market potential, costs, and profitability of the new product.
   - **Example:** Anjali analyzed the cost of materials, pricing, and expected sales to determine the financial feasibility of her new product line.
5. **Product Development:** Creating the actual product.
   - **Example:** Anjali began full-scale production of her new line after successful testing and analysis.
6. **Market Testing:** Introducing the product in a limited area to test its reception.
   - **Example:** Anjali launched her new pottery line in a few select stores to gather feedback before a wider release.
7. **Commercialization:** Full-scale production and marketing of the product.
   - **Example:** After successful market testing, Anjali launched her new collection across all her distribution channels.

2. Innovation and Continuous Improvement:

Innovation involves not just the creation of entirely new products but also the improvement and refinement of existing products to meet changing consumer needs and preferences.

- **Example:** Anjali continuously experimented with new glazing techniques and materials to enhance the quality and appeal of her pottery, ensuring that her products remained fresh and relevant in the market.

6.6 Practical Activity: Designing Your Product Line

Activity Name: The Artisan's Portfolio

- **Setup:** Students will be assigned to groups and each group will take on the role of a company that specializes in a specific product category (e.g., handcrafted goods, tech gadgets, or fashion accessories). Each group will design a product line, making decisions about product attributes, branding, packaging, and product line management.
- **Task:** Groups will decide on the length and depth of their product line, determine whether to fill or stretch the product line, and create a branding and packaging strategy for their products.
- **Presentation:** Each group will present their product line to the class, explaining their decisions and how they plan to position their products in the market.
- **Discussion:** The class will discuss the challenges and opportunities associated with managing a product line, and how different strategies can impact brand identity and customer satisfaction.

6.7 Crafting a Cohesive Collection

As Rohit closed his notebook, he realized that product and product line decisions were not just about creating more items but about crafting a cohesive collection that resonated with customers. Every decision, from the attributes of a single product to the management of the entire product line, had to be carefully considered to maintain the brand's identity and meet the needs of the market.

Rohit knew that by understanding the art of product and product line decisions, he and Anjali could continue to expand their offerings while staying true to the values that made their brand special. Just as a master artisan carefully selects each piece of clay, shapes it, and adds it to a collection, so too must a business carefully curate its products to create a harmonious and successful product line.

CHAPTER VIII

Mastering Branding Decisions – Crafting an Identity

The Story of the Sapphire Jewelers

In the bustling markets of Jaipur, where the air is thick with the scent of spices and the vibrant colors of textiles, there was a small jewelry store named Sapphire Jewelers. The shop was run by Aisha, a young entrepreneur who had inherited the business from her father. Although her jewelry was of exceptional quality, Sapphire Jewelers struggled to stand out among the numerous jewelry stores lining the streets.

One evening, after a slow day at the shop, Aisha sat down with her father, a retired jeweler with decades of experience. "Father, why isn't our store as popular as the others? Our jewels are just as beautiful, if not more," Aisha asked, her voice tinged with frustration.

Her father smiled gently and said, "Aisha, it's not enough to have the best jewels. You need to create a story, an identity, something that resonates with people and makes them feel connected to your brand. This is what branding is all about."

Inspired by her father's wisdom, Aisha embarked on a journey to transform Sapphire Jewelers from a simple shop into a powerful brand that customers would recognize, trust, and love.

7.1 What is Branding?

Aisha's First Lesson:

As Aisha began to explore the world of branding, she learned that **branding** is the process of creating a unique name, design, symbol, or identity that distinguishes a product or service from its competitors. Branding is not just about logos or slogans; it's about the perception that customers have about a product and the emotional connection they feel toward it.

Meaning of Branding:

Branding is the process of developing a distinct identity for a product, service, or company that differentiates it from competitors and builds a lasting image in the minds of consumers. It encompasses the creation of a brand name, logo, tagline, and overall brand experience.

Famous Definitions of Branding:

1. **Philip Kotler:***"Branding is the process of endowing products and services with the power of a brand."*
2. **Significance:** Kotler's definition highlights the idea that branding gives products and services a unique identity and power in the market.
3. **David Aaker:***"A brand is a distinguishing name and/or symbol (such as a logo, trademark, or package design) intended to identify the goods or services of either one seller or a group of sellers, and to differentiate those goods or services from those of competitors."*
4. **Significance:** Aaker emphasizes the role of branding in differentiation and identification, key factors in establishing a brand's market presence.

Importance of Branding Decisions:

Branding decisions are crucial because they determine how a product or service is perceived by the market. Effective branding can lead to strong brand recognition, customer loyalty, and competitive advantage.

1. **Creating a Strong Brand Identity:**
    - Branding helps create a distinct identity that sets a product or company apart from competitors.
    - **Example:** Aisha decided to position Sapphire Jewelers as a brand that offered not just jewelry but timeless pieces of art inspired by Jaipur's rich heritage.
2. **Building Customer Loyalty:**
    - A well-established brand fosters trust and loyalty among customers, encouraging repeat purchases and word-of-mouth recommendations.
    - **Example:** By consistently delivering high-quality products and exceptional service, Sapphire Jewelers built a loyal customer base that returned for every special occasion.
3. **Enhancing Perceived Value:**
    - A strong brand can enhance the perceived value of a product, allowing companies to command higher prices.
    - **Example:** Aisha was able to price her jewelry at a premium because her customers associated the Sapphire Jewelers brand with exclusivity and luxury.
4. **Achieving Market Differentiation:**
    - Branding differentiates a product or service from others in the market, making it easier for customers to choose it over competitors.
    - **Example:** Sapphire Jewelers stood out from other jewelry stores by emphasizing its commitment to craftsmanship and the unique cultural stories behind each piece.

7.2 Elements of a Brand

As Aisha delved deeper, she realized that a brand is composed of several key elements, each contributing to the overall brand identity and perception.

1. Brand Name:

The brand name is the verbal component of the brand that identifies and differentiates a product or service. It should be memorable, meaningful, and easy to pronounce.

- **Example:** Aisha chose the name "Sapphire Jewelers" to evoke images of precious gems and to convey a sense of luxury and exclusivity.

2. Brand Logo:

The brand logo is a visual symbol or design that represents the brand. It should be simple, recognizable, and reflective of the brand's values and identity.

- **Example:** Aisha designed a logo for Sapphire Jewelers featuring a stylized sapphire gemstone, which symbolized the brand's focus on timeless beauty and quality.

3. Brand Slogan or Tagline:

A brand slogan or tagline is a short, memorable phrase that captures the essence of the brand's promise or positioning.

- **Example:** Aisha developed the tagline "Jewels of Timeless Elegance" to reinforce the idea that Sapphire Jewelers offered more than just jewelry—it offered heirlooms that would be cherished for generations.

4. Brand Colors and Typography:

Brand colors and typography are visual elements that contribute to the brand's identity. They should be consistent across all brand communications and align with the brand's personality.

- **Example:** Sapphire Jewelers used deep blue and gold in its branding, colors that conveyed luxury, sophistication, and trust.

5. Brand Voice and Personality:

The brand voice is the tone and style of communication used by the brand, while brand personality refers to the human traits associated with the brand.

- **Example:** Aisha chose a warm, welcoming brand voice for Sapphire Jewelers, with a personality that was both elegant and approachable, reflecting the brand's commitment to customer care.

6. Brand Story:

The brand story is the narrative that communicates the brand's history, values, mission, and what it stands for. It connects emotionally with customers and makes the brand more relatable.

- **Example:** Sapphire Jewelers' brand story highlighted its heritage as a family-owned business rooted in Jaipur's rich tradition of craftsmanship, emphasizing the generational knowledge passed down through the years.

7.3 Branding Strategies

Aisha learned that to build a successful brand, she needed to adopt specific branding strategies that aligned with her business goals and market conditions.

1. Brand Positioning:

Brand positioning is the process of placing a brand in the minds of consumers relative to competing brands. It defines how the brand is different and why it is the better choice.

- **Example:** Aisha positioned Sapphire Jewelers as a premium brand offering exclusive, handcrafted jewelry that celebrated Jaipur's cultural heritage, differentiating it from mass-market jewelry brands.

2. Brand Extension:

Brand extension involves using an established brand name to introduce new products or services in different categories or markets.

- **Example:** After establishing Sapphire Jewelers, Aisha extended the brand to include a line of luxury watches, capitalizing on the brand's reputation for quality and craftsmanship.

3. Co-Branding:

Co-branding is a strategy where two or more brands collaborate to create a new product or service, leveraging the strengths of each brand.

- **Example:** Sapphire Jewelers partnered with a renowned designer to create a limited-edition jewelry collection, combining the designer's fashion expertise with the brand's craftsmanship.

4. Brand Licensing:
Brand licensing involves allowing another company to use the brand's name, logo, or other elements in exchange for a fee or royalty.

- **Example:** Aisha licensed the Sapphire Jewelers brand to a high-end department store, allowing them to sell exclusive jewelry collections under the Sapphire brand name.

5. Private Label Branding:
Private label branding involves selling products under a retailer's own brand name rather than the manufacturer's brand.

- **Example:** Aisha considered offering a private label line of jewelry for a luxury retailer, providing her designs under the retailer's brand name.

6. Multi-Brand Strategy:
A multi-brand strategy involves marketing multiple brands within the same product category, each targeting a different market segment.

- **Example:** Aisha launched a second brand, "Jaipur Gems," targeting a younger, trend-conscious audience, while Sapphire Jewelers continued to focus on the premium, luxury market.

7. Global Branding:
Global branding involves creating a consistent brand identity and strategy across multiple international markets.

- **Example:** As Sapphire Jewelers grew, Aisha explored opportunities to expand into international markets, ensuring that the brand's core identity remained consistent while adapting to local preferences.

7.4 Brand Equity: Building and Managing Brand Value

Aisha discovered that building a strong brand requires more than just a logo and a catchy slogan—it involves creating and maintaining **brand equity**. Brand equity refers to the value that a brand adds to a product or service, based on consumer perceptions, associations, and loyalty.

1. Components of Brand Equity:

1. **Brand Awareness:**
   - **Definition:** The extent to which consumers recognize or recall a brand.
   - **Example:** Aisha invested in marketing campaigns to increase brand awareness, ensuring that Sapphire Jewelers was top of mind when customers thought of luxury jewelry.
2. **Brand Associations:**
   - **Definition:** The mental connections that consumers make between a brand and its attributes, benefits, or experiences.

- **Example:** Sapphire Jewelers was associated with craftsmanship, luxury, and cultural heritage, making it a preferred choice for special occasions.

3. **Perceived Quality:**

   - **Definition:** The consumer's perception of the quality of a brand's products or services compared to competitors.
   - **Example:** Aisha ensured that every piece of jewelry met the highest standards of quality, reinforcing the perception of Sapphire Jewelers as a premium brand.

4. **Brand Loyalty:**

   - **Definition:** The extent to which consumers continue to purchase the same brand over time, despite competition.
   - **Example:** Sapphire Jewelers built strong brand loyalty by consistently delivering exceptional customer service and exclusive designs.

5. **Brand Assets:**

   - **Definition:** Patents, trademarks, and other proprietary rights associated with the brand that add to its value.
   - **Example:** Aisha protected the Sapphire Jewelers brand name and logo through trademarks, ensuring that no other company could use them.

2. Measuring Brand Equity:

To effectively manage brand equity, Aisha needed to measure it regularly. Common methods for measuring brand equity include:

- **Brand Audits:** Comprehensive reviews of the brand's performance and market position.
- **Customer Surveys:** Gathering feedback on brand perception, loyalty, and satisfaction.
- **Sales Analysis:** Monitoring sales trends to assess the impact of branding efforts.
- **Market Share Analysis:** Evaluating the brand's share of the market compared to competitors.

3. Managing Brand Equity:

Managing brand equity involves maintaining and enhancing the value of the brand over time. This requires consistent branding, innovation, and adapting to changing market conditions.

- **Example:** Aisha regularly refreshed Sapphire Jewelers' marketing campaigns and introduced new collections to keep the brand relevant and appealing to both existing and new customers.

7.5 Brand Architecture: Organizing the Brand Portfolio

As Sapphire Jewelers expanded, Aisha needed to consider how to organize and manage her growing portfolio of brands. **Brand architecture** is the structure of brands within an organization, determining how the brands relate to each other and to the parent brand.

1. Types of Brand Architecture:

1. **Branded House (Monolithic):**

- **Definition:** A single master brand is used across all products and services.
- **Example:** Aisha initially used a branded house strategy, with all products and services under the Sapphire Jewelers brand.

2. **House of Brands (Pluralistic):**

    - **Definition:** Each product or service has its own unique brand, with little or no connection to the parent brand.
    - **Example:** If Aisha had launched a completely separate brand for watches, with no visible connection to Sapphire Jewelers, it would be a house of brands strategy.

3. **Endorsed Brands:**

    - **Definition:** Individual brands are distinct but are endorsed by the parent brand.
    - **Example:** Aisha introduced "Sapphire Luxe," a high-end collection endorsed by the main Sapphire Jewelers brand, which lent credibility to the new line.

4. **Sub-Brands:**

    - **Definition:** A master brand supports a variety of related products or services with sub-brands.
    - **Example:** "Sapphire Bridal" became a sub-brand under Sapphire Jewelers, offering a specialized line of wedding jewelry.

2. Choosing the Right Brand Architecture:

The choice of brand architecture depends on the company's goals, target markets, and the relationship between the brands.

- **Example:** Aisha chose a branded house strategy for Sapphire Jewelers to maintain a unified brand identity, but as she expanded into different market segments, she introduced sub-brands to cater to specific customer needs.

3. Benefits of Effective Brand Architecture:

- **Clarity:** Helps customers understand the brand's offerings and relationships between products.
- **Efficiency:** Streamlines marketing efforts and resources across the brand portfolio.
- **Growth:** Allows for strategic expansion and introduction of new products or services.

7.6 Practical Activity: Building Your Brand

Activity Name: Crafting a Brand Identity

- **Setup:** Students will be divided into groups, and each group will create a brand for a fictional company in a specific industry (e.g., fashion, technology, food and beverage). Each group will develop the key elements of their brand, including the brand name, logo, slogan, colors, and brand story.
- **Task:** Groups will present their brand identity to the class, explaining how they positioned the brand, the target audience, and the branding strategies they used. They will also discuss how they would build and manage brand equity over time.
- **Presentation:** Each group will showcase their brand identity and explain their branding decisions, followed by a discussion on the potential challenges and opportunities their brand might face in the market.

7.7 The Power of a Strong Brand

As Aisha looked around her newly rebranded store, she felt a deep sense of satisfaction. The transformation of Sapphire Jewelers from a small, unnoticed shop to a recognized and beloved brand was not just about changing the logo or the name—it was about creating an identity that resonated with customers on a personal level. Aisha understood that a strong brand is more than just a business asset; it's a story, a promise, and a relationship with the customer.

Through thoughtful branding decisions, Aisha had built something that customers didn't just buy from—they believed in. And with that belief came trust, loyalty, and the power to stand out in a crowded marketplace. As she prepared to welcome her first customer of the day, Aisha knew that the journey of branding was ongoing, requiring constant attention and care. But she was ready, knowing that Sapphire Jewelers would continue to shine brightly for generations to come.

CHAPTER IX

Packaging and Labeling Decisions – Beyond the Box

The Tale of the Sweet Shop

In the vibrant streets of Kolkata, there was a sweet shop named "Bengal Delights" that was famous for its traditional sweets like rasgullas, sandesh, and mishti doi. The shop, run by a family for generations, had a loyal customer base, but it was struggling to attract new customers in the increasingly competitive market.

One day, Priya, the youngest member of the family, who had recently completed her business studies, approached her father with an idea. "Father, our sweets are the best, but they're not standing out. Everyone loves our products once they taste them, but how do we get them to choose us in the first place?"

Her father, experienced but open to new ideas, replied, "Perhaps it's time to think beyond the taste, Priya. We need to make our sweets irresistible even before they are tasted. It's time to rethink how we present them. Maybe the answer lies in how we package and label our sweets."

With this insight, Priya set out to transform Bengal Delights, not just through the quality of their sweets, but through the packaging and labeling that would entice customers and tell the story of their brand.

8.1 The Importance of Packaging and Labeling

Priya's First Step:

Priya learned that **packaging** and **labeling** are crucial components of a product's marketing strategy. They are not just functional but are powerful tools for attracting customers, conveying brand identity, and differentiating a product from competitors.

Meaning of Packaging:

Packaging refers to the process of designing and producing the container or wrapper for a product. It serves multiple purposes, from protecting the product to facilitating its storage, distribution, and sale. More importantly, packaging is the first point of interaction between the product and the consumer, making it a vital element of the overall marketing mix.

Meaning of Labeling:

Labeling involves creating tags or labels that provide information about the product. Labels can include the brand name, product ingredients, usage instructions, nutritional information, and other details. Effective labeling not only informs but also enhances the product's appeal and aligns with the brand's image.

Importance of Packaging and Labeling Decisions:

1. **Attracting Attention:**

    - Packaging is often the first thing a customer notices on the shelf, making it a key factor in influencing purchase decisions.
    - **Example:** Priya decided to redesign the packaging for Bengal Delights' sweets using vibrant, traditional patterns that would catch the eye and reflect the cultural heritage of Bengal.

2. **Conveying Brand Identity:**
    - Packaging and labeling help communicate the brand's values, personality, and story to the consumer.
    - **Example:** The new packaging for Bengal Delights featured a logo with the tagline "Tradition Wrapped in Sweetness," emphasizing the brand's deep roots in Bengali culture.

3. **Differentiating the Product:**
    - Unique packaging and labeling can set a product apart from competitors, making it more recognizable and appealing.
    - **Example:** To stand out from other sweet shops, Priya introduced eco-friendly, reusable packaging that aligned with the growing consumer preference for sustainable products.

4. **Providing Information:**
    - Labels provide essential information about the product, such as ingredients, usage instructions, and expiration dates, which can influence the buying decision.
    - **Example:** Priya added detailed labels to each sweet box, including nutritional information and serving suggestions, making it easier for customers to make informed choices.

5. **Enhancing Perceived Value:**
    - High-quality packaging can enhance the perceived value of the product, allowing the brand to justify premium pricing.
    - **Example:** The new, elegantly designed boxes made Bengal Delights' sweets an ideal choice for gifting, leading to an increase in sales during festive seasons.

8.2 Functions of Packaging

As Priya delved deeper, she realized that packaging serves several important functions, each contributing to the overall success of a product.

1. Protection:

The primary function of packaging is to protect the product from damage, contamination, and spoilage during transportation, storage, and handling.

- **Example:** Priya ensured that the new packaging for Bengal Delights included sturdy, airtight containers that kept the sweets fresh and protected from damage during delivery.

2. Convenience:

Packaging should be designed for convenience, making it easy for consumers to carry, open, use, and dispose of the product.

- **Example:** Priya introduced easy-to-open boxes with resealable lids, making it convenient for customers to enjoy the sweets over several days without compromising freshness.

3. Communication:

Packaging communicates important information about the product, including brand identity, product details, and usage instructions.

- **Example:** The packaging for Bengal Delights featured clear labeling with a description of each sweet, the story behind its creation, and the best way to enjoy it.

4. Safety:

Packaging must ensure that the product is safe for consumption, meeting all regulatory requirements and standards.

- **Example:** Priya made sure that the packaging materials were food-grade and complied with health and safety regulations, ensuring that the sweets were safe to eat.

5. Promotion:

Packaging serves as a silent salesperson, promoting the product and encouraging impulse purchases.

- **Example:** Priya's vibrant and culturally inspired packaging attracted attention on the shelves, leading to higher impulse buys from customers drawn to the brand's aesthetic appeal.

6. Environmental Consideration:

Modern packaging should consider environmental impact, using sustainable materials and minimizing waste.

- **Example:** Priya switched to biodegradable packaging materials for Bengal Delights, aligning with consumer demand for environmentally friendly products and enhancing the brand's reputation.

8.3 Types of Packaging

Priya learned that packaging can be classified into three main types, each serving different purposes in the product's lifecycle.

1. Primary Packaging:

Primary packaging is the packaging that directly contains the product and is in direct contact with it. It is the most important layer of packaging as it protects the product and provides the first visual impression.

- **Example:** The tin canister that holds Bengal Delights' sweets is primary packaging, designed to keep the sweets fresh and protect them from external elements.

2. Secondary Packaging:

Secondary packaging is the outer packaging that holds the primary package. It is often used for branding, providing additional protection, and grouping multiple products together.

- **Example:** The decorative box that contains several tin canisters of sweets is secondary packaging, used for branding and presentation, especially for gifting purposes.

3. Tertiary Packaging:

Tertiary packaging is used for bulk handling, storage, and transportation of products. It typically involves the use of pallets, crates, or cartons.

- **Example:** The large cartons used to transport multiple boxes of Bengal Delights' sweets to retailers are tertiary packaging, ensuring safe delivery without damage.

8.4 Packaging Design Decisions

As Priya worked on revamping Bengal Delights' packaging, she realized that the design decisions she made would significantly impact the product's market performance. Here are the key elements she considered:

1. Material Selection:

Choosing the right material for packaging is crucial for protecting the product, enhancing its appeal, and meeting sustainability goals.

- **Example:** Priya selected tin canisters for primary packaging due to their durability and ability to keep sweets fresh. She chose biodegradable paper for secondary packaging to align with the brand's sustainability focus.

2. Shape and Size:

The shape and size of the packaging should be practical for both the consumer and the retailer, while also reflecting the brand's identity.

- **Example:** Priya opted for a compact, cylindrical shape for the tin canisters, which was easy to store and transport. The size was carefully chosen to offer just the right quantity for gifting.

3. Color and Graphics:

Color and graphics play a crucial role in attracting attention, conveying the brand message, and differentiating the product from competitors.

- **Example:** The packaging for Bengal Delights was designed with traditional Bengali patterns in vibrant colors, making it visually striking and culturally resonant.

4. Typography:

Typography on packaging must be legible, appealing, and aligned with the brand's identity.

- **Example:** Priya used elegant, serif fonts for the brand name and product descriptions, reinforcing the premium and traditional image of Bengal Delights.

5. Innovation:

Innovative packaging can create a unique selling proposition (USP) and enhance the consumer experience.

- **Example:** Priya introduced a reusable tin canister with a decorative lid that could be repurposed as a storage container, adding value to the packaging and making it a keepsake for customers.

8.5 Labeling Decisions

Priya also understood the importance of labeling as part of the packaging strategy. Labels provide essential information and contribute to the overall branding and marketing of the product.

1. Types of Labels:

1. **Brand Label:**

   - A label that carries only the brand name or logo.
   - **Example:** The primary label on Bengal Delights' tin canisters prominently displayed the brand name and logo, ensuring brand recognition.

2. **Descriptive Label:**

   - A label that provides information about the product's usage, features, ingredients, and benefits.
   - **Example:** Each canister had a descriptive label that included the ingredients, nutritional information, and a brief history of the sweet, educating customers about what they were buying.

3. **Grade Label:**

   - A label that indicates the quality or grade of the product.
   - **Example:** Priya introduced a grade label on premium products, such as "Exclusively Handcrafted," to differentiate the top-tier offerings from the standard range.

4. **Informative Label:**

   - A label that provides additional information required by law or that is helpful to consumers, such as expiration dates and storage instructions.
   - **Example:** The bottom of each tin canister included an informative label with the production date, expiration date, and storage instructions to ensure the best quality of the sweets.

2. Legal and Regulatory Considerations:
Priya ensured that all labels complied with local regulations regarding food safety, nutritional information, and other legal requirements.

- **Example:** Bengal Delights' labels met all FSSAI (Food Safety and Standards Authority of India) requirements, including accurate ingredient lists and allergen information, ensuring compliance and consumer trust.

3. Label Design:
The design of the label must be consistent with the overall packaging and brand identity, ensuring that it enhances the product's appeal.

- **Example:** Priya's label design matched the packaging, with consistent colors, fonts, and branding elements, creating a cohesive and attractive presentation.

8.6 The Impact of Technology on Packaging and Labeling

Priya recognized that technology plays a significant role in modern packaging and labeling, offering new opportunities for innovation and efficiency.

1. Smart Packaging:
Smart packaging uses technology to provide additional features, such as freshness indicators, QR codes, and interactive experiences.

- **Example:** Priya introduced QR codes on Bengal Delights' packaging that customers could scan to learn more about the origins of the sweets, watch videos on how they were made, and access special offers.

2. Sustainable Packaging Technologies:

Advancements in sustainable materials and processes have enabled more environmentally friendly packaging solutions.

- **Example:** Bengal Delights adopted sustainable packaging materials that were biodegradable and sourced from renewable resources, reducing the brand's environmental footprint.

3. Digital Labeling:

Digital labeling allows for dynamic, customizable labels that can be easily updated or personalized for different markets or promotions.

- **Example:** Priya explored the idea of using digital labels for limited-edition products, allowing for quick customization and personalization, such as adding a customer's name to the packaging.

8.7 Practical Activity: Packaging and Labeling Workshop

Activity Name: Designing the Perfect Package

- **Setup:** Students will be divided into groups and each group will be assigned a fictional product. Their task is to design both the packaging and labeling for their product, considering factors like protection, convenience, branding, and sustainability.
- **Task:** Groups will present their packaging and labeling designs to the class, explaining the decisions they made and how their designs will attract and inform customers. They should also discuss how technology could enhance their packaging and labeling.
- **Presentation:** Each group will showcase their packaging and labeling designs, followed by a class discussion on the effectiveness and potential challenges of their strategies.

8.8 Packaging – The Silent Salesperson

As Priya walked through the newly refurbished Bengal Delights, she felt a sense of pride. The sweets that her family had lovingly crafted for generations were now presented in a way that did justice to their quality and heritage. The new packaging and labeling were not just about aesthetics—they told a story, connected with customers, and made the products irresistible even before they were tasted.

Priya realized that packaging and labeling were powerful tools in the world of marketing, acting as the silent salesperson that influenced customer decisions. Through careful planning and creativity, she had successfully transformed the look and feel of Bengal Delights, ensuring that the brand stood out in a crowded market and continued to delight customers for years to come.

CHAPTER X

The Product Life Cycle Concept – Navigating the Journey from Introduction to Decline

The Story of the Evergreen Tree

In a quaint village nestled in the hills of Himachal Pradesh, there was a small shop called Evergreen Crafts, known for its hand-carved wooden toys. The shop had been in the family for generations, and each generation had added something new to the collection. But as time passed, the demand for wooden toys began to wane, and the once-thriving business faced challenges in attracting new customers.

Ravi, the youngest member of the family, had recently taken over the shop. He noticed that some toys sold well, while others remained on the shelves for months. Curious to understand why, Ravi spoke to his grandfather, who had seen the business through both its peak and its lean years.

"Grandfather," Ravi asked, "Why do some of our toys sell out quickly while others don't seem to interest people anymore? How do we know when it's time to create something new or let go of the old?"

His grandfather, a wise and experienced craftsman, replied, "Every product, just like every living thing, has a life cycle. Understanding this cycle can help us decide when to nurture, when to innovate, and when to say goodbye. This is the concept of the product life cycle."

Inspired by his grandfather's words, Ravi set out to learn about the Product Life Cycle (PLC) and how it could help Evergreen Crafts navigate the changing tides of business.

9.1 What is the Product Life Cycle (PLC)?

Ravi's First Lesson:

Ravi learned that the **Product Life Cycle (PLC)** is a concept that describes the stages a product goes through from its introduction to the market until its eventual decline and withdrawal. Understanding the PLC helps businesses make informed decisions about product development, marketing strategies, and resource allocation at different stages.

Meaning of Product Life Cycle:

The Product Life Cycle (PLC) refers to the progression of a product through four key stages: introduction, growth, maturity, and decline. Each stage is characterized by different challenges and opportunities, and requires distinct marketing strategies to optimize the product's success in the market.

Famous Definitions of Product Life Cycle:

1. **Philip Kotler:***"The product life cycle is an important concept in marketing. It describes the stages a product goes through from when it was first thought of until it finally is removed from the market."*
2. **Significance:** Kotler's definition emphasizes the PLC as a framework for understanding the lifespan of a product in the market and its implications for marketing strategy.
3. **William J. Stanton:***"The product life cycle is the course that a product's sales and profits take over its lifetime."*
4. **Significance:** Stanton highlights the impact of the PLC on a product's sales and profitability, key indicators that guide business decisions.

Importance of Understanding the Product Life Cycle:

1. **Strategic Planning:**
   - The PLC provides a roadmap for businesses to plan their marketing, production, and financial strategies over time.
   - **Example:** Ravi used the PLC to identify when Evergreen Crafts' toys were in the maturity stage, signaling the need to innovate or refresh the product line.
2. **Resource Allocation:**
   - By understanding the PLC, businesses can allocate resources more effectively, investing in growth opportunities and scaling back during decline.
   - **Example:** Ravi decided to focus marketing efforts on newly introduced toys in the growth stage, while reducing investment in toys that were in the decline stage.
3. **Product Innovation:**
   - The PLC encourages businesses to innovate and develop new products as existing ones reach the end of their life cycle.
   - **Example:** As some of the traditional wooden toys reached the decline stage, Ravi began exploring new designs and materials to attract modern consumers.
4. **Competitive Advantage:**
   - Businesses that effectively manage the PLC can gain a competitive advantage by extending the life cycle of their products and staying ahead of market trends.
   - **Example:** By refreshing product designs and introducing limited-edition collections, Evergreen Crafts kept its brand relevant and competitive in the market.

9.2 Stages of the Product Life Cycle

Ravi learned that the Product Life Cycle is divided into four distinct stages, each with its own characteristics, challenges, and strategies.

1. Introduction Stage:

The introduction stage is when a new product is launched into the market. Sales are typically low, and the focus is on building awareness and attracting early adopters.

- **Characteristics:**
  - Low sales and high costs.
  - High levels of marketing and promotional expenses.
  - Limited distribution channels.
  - Focus on educating the market about the product.
- **Strategies:**
  - Invest heavily in marketing to build awareness and generate interest.
  - Price the product competitively or offer introductory promotions to encourage trial.

  - Focus on product quality and unique features to differentiate from competitors.

- **Example:** When Evergreen Crafts introduced a new line of eco-friendly toys, Ravi invested in marketing campaigns that highlighted the sustainability of the products, targeting environmentally conscious parents.

2. Growth Stage:

The growth stage is characterized by a rapid increase in sales as the product gains market acceptance. Profits begin to rise, and the product becomes more widely available.

- **Characteristics:**
  - Rapid sales growth and increasing profits.
  - Expanding distribution channels.
  - Growing brand recognition and customer base.
  - Entry of competitors into the market.
- **Strategies:**
  - Expand distribution to reach a broader audience.
  - Introduce product variations or improvements to maintain interest.
  - Invest in brand building to establish loyalty and differentiate from competitors.
- **Example:** As the eco-friendly toys gained popularity, Ravi expanded distribution to online platforms and introduced new designs to keep the product line fresh and appealing.

3. Maturity Stage:

The maturity stage is when the product reaches peak market penetration. Sales growth slows, and the market becomes saturated with competitors.

- **Characteristics:**
  - Slowing sales growth and stabilizing profits.
  - High competition leading to price pressure.
  - Market saturation with few new customer segments to capture.
  - Focus on maintaining market share and extending the product's life.
- **Strategies:**
  - Focus on product differentiation through branding, quality, and customer service.
  - Implement cost-saving measures to maintain profitability.
  - Explore new markets or customer segments to sustain sales.
  - Consider product enhancements or updates to reignite interest.
- **Example:** To extend the life of its popular toys, Evergreen Crafts introduced limited-edition versions and enhanced packaging, targeting collectors and gift buyers.

4. Decline Stage:

The decline stage occurs when the product's sales and profits begin to fall. This can happen due to changes in consumer preferences, technological advancements, or the introduction of superior competing products.

- **Characteristics:**
    - Declining sales and shrinking profits.
    - Decreased market interest and relevance.
    - Reduction in marketing and production efforts.
    - Focus on phasing out or repositioning the product.
- **Strategies:**
    - Reduce production and marketing costs to maximize remaining profits.
    - Consider discontinuing the product or phasing it out gradually.
    - Explore opportunities for product repositioning or finding niche markets.
    - Plan for product replacement or innovation to fill the gap.
- **Example:** As demand for traditional wooden toys declined, Ravi reduced production and began phasing out older designs, while investing in new, modern toys that appealed to contemporary tastes.

9.3 Variations of the Product Life Cycle

Ravi discovered that not all products follow the standard PLC pattern. Some products experience variations in their life cycle, requiring different strategies.

1. Fads:

Fads are products that experience rapid growth and decline in a short period. They become popular quickly but fall out of favor just as fast.

- **Example:** A limited-edition toy based on a popular movie might see a surge in sales immediately after the movie's release, but interest could wane quickly as the trend passes.

2. Fashion Products:

Fashion products have recurring life cycles as styles and trends come and go. They may go through cycles of popularity, decline, and resurgence.

- **Example:** Evergreen Crafts noticed that some traditional toy designs became popular again as retro or vintage styles became trendy, leading to a revival in sales.

3. Seasonal Products:

Seasonal products experience predictable sales patterns based on the time of year. They peak during specific seasons and decline during off-seasons.

- **Example:** During festivals like Diwali or Christmas, Evergreen Crafts' sales of decorative toys and gift sets peaked, while sales slowed down during the rest of the year.

4. Extended Maturity:

Some products achieve an extended maturity stage, maintaining steady sales over a long period without significant decline.

- **Example:** Ravi found that certain classic toys with timeless appeal, such as wooden trains, continued to sell well for years, maintaining a long maturity stage.

9.4 Strategies for Each Stage of the Product Life Cycle

Ravi realized that each stage of the PLC requires tailored strategies to maximize the product's potential and ensure long-term success.

1. Strategies for the Introduction Stage:

- **Product Development:** Focus on ensuring product quality and uniqueness.
- **Pricing:** Consider penetration pricing to attract customers or skimming pricing to maximize early profits.
- **Promotion:** Invest heavily in marketing and promotional activities to build awareness.
- **Distribution:** Start with selective distribution to target early adopters.

2. Strategies for the Growth Stage:

- **Product Diversification:** Introduce new variations or related products to capitalize on growth.
- **Pricing:** Gradually increase prices if demand is strong or reduce prices to fend off competitors.
- **Promotion:** Shift focus from awareness to brand building and customer retention.
- **Distribution:** Expand distribution channels to reach a wider audience.

3. Strategies for the Maturity Stage:

- **Product Enhancement:** Innovate or improve the product to differentiate it from competitors.
- **Pricing:** Implement competitive pricing strategies to maintain market share.
- **Promotion:** Focus on reinforcing brand loyalty and emphasizing product benefits.
- **Distribution:** Maximize distribution efficiency and explore new markets.

4. Strategies for the Decline Stage:

- **Product Rationalization:** Phase out weak products and focus on profitable ones.
- **Pricing:** Lower prices to clear inventory or maintain profitability for niche markets.
- **Promotion:** Reduce marketing expenses and target specific customer segments.
- **Distribution:** Scale back distribution and focus on cost-effective channels.

9.5 Extending the Product Life Cycle

Ravi wanted to explore ways to extend the life cycle of Evergreen Crafts' toys, ensuring they remained relevant and profitable for as long as possible.

1. Product Innovation:

Introduce new features, designs, or technologies to refresh the product and attract new customers.

- **Example:** Ravi experimented with adding interactive elements to traditional toys, such as sound and movement, to appeal to tech-savvy children.

2. Market Expansion:
Explore new markets, both geographically and demographically, to extend the product's reach.

- **Example:** Evergreen Crafts expanded its distribution to international markets, where there was growing interest in traditional Indian toys.

3. Repositioning:
Reposition the product to target a different market segment or fulfill a different need.

- **Example:** Ravi repositioned certain toys as educational tools for early childhood development, appealing to parents and educators.

4. Product Line Extension:
Introduce new products within the same category to create a comprehensive product line, enhancing the appeal of the original product.

- **Example:** By introducing matching sets of toys and accessories, Evergreen Crafts encouraged customers to purchase multiple items, extending the life cycle of each product.

5. Marketing Revitalization:
Refresh the marketing strategy to reignite interest in the product, such as launching new campaigns, rebranding, or updating packaging.

- **Example:** Ravi launched a nostalgic marketing campaign that highlighted the heritage and craftsmanship of Evergreen Crafts' toys, attracting both new customers and former ones who fondly remembered the brand.

9.6 Practical Activity: Mapping the Product Life Cycle

Activity Name: The Life Cycle Journey

- **Setup:** Students will be divided into groups, and each group will choose a product (real or fictional). They will map out the product's life cycle, identifying the current stage and developing strategies for each stage.
- **Task:** Groups will present their product life cycle maps, explaining how they would manage the product at each stage to maximize its success. They will also suggest ways to extend the life cycle of the product.
- **Presentation:** Each group will present their findings to the class, followed by a discussion on the challenges and opportunities associated with managing a product through its life cycle.

9.7 Navigating the Product Journey

As Ravi sat back and reflected on what he had learned, he understood that the Product Life Cycle is more than just a theoretical concept—it's a practical tool that can guide businesses through the highs and lows of the market. By understanding the different stages of the PLC, Ravi could make more informed decisions about when to invest, when to innovate, and when to gracefully retire a product.

The success of Evergreen Crafts didn't just depend on the quality of the toys, but on Ravi's ability to navigate the product journey from introduction to decline. With the knowledge of the Product Life Cycle, Ravi was confident that he could keep the family business thriving for generations to come, just like the evergreen trees that inspired its name.

CHAPTER XI

New Product Development – From Concept to Market

The Inventor's Challenge

In the bustling city of Pune, where innovation and tradition walk hand in hand, lived an inventor named Arjun. Known for his creative mind, Arjun had a small workshop where he tinkered with gadgets and tools, always searching for the next big idea. Despite his talent, Arjun faced a challenge that many inventors do—turning a bright idea into a successful product.

One day, while working on a new kitchen gadget, Arjun's friend Meera, a successful entrepreneur, visited him. "Arjun," she said, "Your ideas are brilliant, but you often struggle to get them to market. Have you thought about following a structured process to develop your products?"

Arjun, always eager to learn, replied, "I've heard about new product development, but it seems complicated. Can you help me understand how to bring my ideas to life in a way that ensures success?"

Meera smiled and agreed to guide Arjun through the process of New Product Development (NPD), a journey that would take him from the spark of an idea to a market-ready product.

10.1 What is New Product Development (NPD)?

Arjun's First Lesson:

Arjun learned that **New Product Development (NPD)** is a systematic process that takes an idea from concept to market. It involves several stages, each critical for ensuring that the product not only meets market needs but also stands out from the competition. Successful NPD requires careful planning, creativity, and execution to transform an idea into a profitable product.

Meaning of New Product Development:

New Product Development (NPD) is the process of bringing a new product or service to the market. It includes ideation, design, development, testing, and commercialization. NPD is essential for businesses to innovate, grow, and remain competitive in a dynamic market environment.

Famous Definitions of New Product Development:

1. **Philip Kotler:***"New product development is the development of original products, product improvements, product modifications, and new brands through the firm's own research and development efforts."*
2. **Significance:** Kotler's definition highlights the various aspects of NPD, including innovation, improvement, and branding, all of which contribute to a company's growth.
3. **Crawford and Di Benedetto:***"New Product Development is the process of creating a new product or improving an existing one, including the stages from concept to commercialization."*
4. **Significance:** This definition emphasizes the structured process of NPD, from the initial concept through to market launch, ensuring that each stage is carefully managed.

Importance of New Product Development:

1. **Driving Innovation:**
    - NPD is crucial for innovation, allowing businesses to introduce new solutions that meet changing consumer needs and market trends.

- **Example:** Arjun's kitchen gadget, designed to simplify cooking, was an innovative solution that addressed a common problem faced by many home cooks.

2. **Maintaining Competitiveness:**

   - In a competitive market, businesses must continually develop new products to stay relevant and capture market share.
   - **Example:** By developing new products regularly, Arjun could keep his brand fresh and competitive, ensuring that his workshop remained a go-to destination for innovative gadgets.

3. **Meeting Consumer Needs:**

   - NPD enables companies to respond to evolving consumer preferences, ensuring that their products remain relevant and desirable.
   - **Example:** Arjun's kitchen gadget was designed with input from potential users, ensuring that it met their needs and preferences.

4. **Enhancing Business Growth:**

   - New products can open up new revenue streams, attract new customers, and expand the business's market presence.
   - **Example:** The success of Arjun's new kitchen gadget allowed him to expand his business, launching a line of related products and entering new markets.

10.2 The Stages of New Product Development

Meera explained to Arjun that New Product Development is a structured process with several key stages. Each stage requires careful planning and execution to ensure the product's success.

1. Idea Generation:

The NPD process begins with idea generation, where new product concepts are created. Ideas can come from various sources, including customers, employees, competitors, and market research.

- **Sources of Ideas:**

  - **Internal Sources:** Employees, research and development teams, and brainstorming sessions.
  - **External Sources:** Customers, competitors, market trends, and suppliers.
  - **Example:** Arjun's idea for the kitchen gadget came from observing his own challenges in the kitchen and listening to feedback from friends and family.

2. Idea Screening:

Once ideas are generated, the next step is idea screening, where potential ideas are evaluated to determine their feasibility and alignment with business goals. This stage helps filter out unviable ideas early on.

- **Criteria for Screening:**

  - Market potential.
  - Alignment with business strategy.

- Feasibility in terms of technology and cost.
- **Example:** Arjun used a simple scoring system to evaluate each idea, focusing on the potential market size and ease of manufacturing.

3. Concept Development and Testing:

In this stage, the selected ideas are developed into detailed product concepts. These concepts are then tested with target customers to gather feedback and refine the product idea.

- **Concept Development:**
  - Defining the product features, benefits, and target market.
  - Creating detailed product specifications and prototypes.
  - **Example:** Arjun developed a prototype of his kitchen gadget and presented it to a focus group of home cooks to get their feedback.
- **Concept Testing:**
  - Gathering feedback from potential customers on the product concept.
  - Making adjustments based on feedback to improve the product's appeal.
  - **Example:** Based on feedback, Arjun made changes to the design, making the gadget more user-friendly and adding features that customers suggested.

4. Business Analysis:

The business analysis stage involves evaluating the financial viability of the product. This includes estimating costs, pricing, sales projections, and profitability.

- **Key Elements of Business Analysis:**
  - Cost estimation (production, marketing, distribution).
  - Pricing strategy.
  - Sales forecasting and breakeven analysis.
  - **Example:** Arjun calculated the costs of producing his kitchen gadget, set a competitive price, and estimated how many units he needed to sell to break even and make a profit.

5. Product Development:

In the product development stage, the product concept is transformed into a tangible product. This involves designing the product, creating prototypes, and preparing for mass production.

- **Steps in Product Development:**
  - Detailed product design and engineering.
  - Prototype development and testing.
  - Finalizing manufacturing processes.
  - **Example:** Arjun worked with a design team to create the final version of his kitchen gadget, ensuring it was ready for mass production.

6. Market Testing:

Market testing involves introducing the product to a limited market to gauge its performance before a full-scale launch. This stage helps identify potential issues and make final adjustments.

- **Types of Market Testing:**
    - **Test Marketing:** Selling the product in a limited geographic area or market segment to assess its performance.
    - **Controlled Test Markets:** Testing the product in a controlled environment, such as select stores or online platforms.
    - **Simulated Test Markets:** Using virtual or simulated environments to test customer responses.
    - **Example:** Arjun launched his kitchen gadget in select stores in Pune, gathering data on customer reactions, sales performance, and potential improvements.

7. Commercialization:

The final stage of NPD is commercialization, where the product is launched on a full scale. This involves ramping up production, implementing marketing campaigns, and distributing the product widely.

- **Steps in Commercialization:**
    - Full-scale production and distribution.
    - Launching marketing and promotional campaigns.
    - Monitoring sales and customer feedback.
    - **Example:** After successful market testing, Arjun launched his kitchen gadget across major cities in India, supported by an online marketing campaign and strategic partnerships with retailers.

10.3 Challenges in New Product Development

Arjun also learned that NPD is not without its challenges. Many products fail to succeed due to various pitfalls along the way.

1. High Costs and Risk:

Developing a new product can be expensive, with significant investments required in research, development, marketing, and production. There's also the risk that the product may not succeed in the market.

- **Example:** Arjun faced high upfront costs in designing and prototyping his kitchen gadget, with the uncertainty of whether it would be well-received by consumers.

2. Market Uncertainty:

Predicting how a new product will perform in the market is challenging. Market conditions, consumer preferences, and competition can change rapidly, affecting the product's success.

- **Example:** Despite thorough market research, Arjun was unsure if his gadget would appeal to a broad audience or be overshadowed by competitors.

3. Technical Challenges:

Developing a new product often involves technical challenges, such as manufacturing issues, quality control, and integrating new technologies.

- **Example:** Arjun encountered difficulties in sourcing materials that met the quality standards required for his gadget, leading to delays in production.

4. Managing Innovation:
Balancing innovation with practicality is a challenge in NPD. Overly ambitious ideas may be technically unfeasible or too costly, while conservative ideas may fail to stand out in the market.

- **Example:** Arjun had to find a balance between incorporating innovative features in his gadget and ensuring it was affordable and easy to use.

5. Time to Market:
Bringing a new product to market quickly is often critical for capitalizing on opportunities and beating competitors. Delays in the NPD process can result in missed opportunities.

- **Example:** Arjun worked against the clock to launch his gadget before a major competitor introduced a similar product, ensuring he captured the first-mover advantage.

10.4 Best Practices for Successful New Product Development

To overcome these challenges, Meera shared some best practices with Arjun for successful NPD.

1. Customer-Centric Approach:
Focus on understanding and meeting the needs of the target customer. Involve customers early in the process through surveys, focus groups, and beta testing.

- **Example:** Arjun's success with his kitchen gadget was due in part to his continuous engagement with potential users, ensuring the final product met their needs and expectations.

2. Cross-Functional Collaboration:
Involve teams from different departments (e.g., marketing, engineering, finance) in the NPD process to ensure all aspects of the product are considered.

- **Example:** Arjun collaborated with designers, engineers, and marketers to develop a product that was not only functional but also appealing and marketable.

3. Agile Development:
Use an agile approach to NPD, allowing for flexibility, quick iterations, and continuous improvement based on feedback.

- **Example:** Arjun adopted an agile approach, making rapid changes to his gadget's design based on prototype testing and user feedback, resulting in a better final product.

4. Thorough Market Research:
Conduct extensive market research to understand customer needs, market trends, and the competitive landscape before and during the NPD process.

- **Example:** Arjun's market research helped him identify a gap in the market for user-friendly kitchen gadgets, guiding the development of his product.

5. Clear Objectives and Milestones:

Set clear objectives and milestones for each stage of the NPD process, ensuring the project stays on track and meets its goals.

- **Example:** Arjun set specific milestones, such as completing the prototype by a certain date and launching the product within six months, which helped him manage the project effectively.

10.5 Practical Activity: Developing a New Product

Activity Name: From Idea to Launch

- **Setup:** Students will be divided into groups, and each group will work through the New Product Development process for a fictional product. They will generate ideas, screen them, develop a concept, conduct a business analysis, and create a prototype plan.
- **Task:** Groups will present their new product ideas to the class, explaining how they navigated each stage of the NPD process. They will also discuss potential challenges they might face and how they would address them.
- **Presentation:** Each group will showcase their new product concept, complete with a prototype plan, business analysis, and marketing strategy, followed by a discussion on the feasibility and potential success of the product.

10.6 Turning Ideas into Reality

As Arjun completed his journey through the New Product Development process, he realized that bringing a product to market is much more than just having a great idea. It requires careful planning, collaboration, and a deep understanding of the market and customer needs. With the right approach, even the most challenging ideas can be transformed into successful products that resonate with consumers.

Through the guidance of Meera and his newfound knowledge of NPD, Arjun successfully launched his kitchen gadget, earning praise from customers and establishing himself as a successful inventor and entrepreneur. He knew that this was just the beginning—there were many more ideas waiting to be brought to life, each with the potential to become the next big thing in the market.

CHAPTER XII

Pricing Decisions – The Art and Science of Value

The Merchant's Dilemma

In the vibrant city of Delhi, where markets bustle with activity and traders haggle over prices, there was a merchant named Rakesh who owned a successful spice shop. His shop, "Spice World," was known for its wide variety of high-quality spices sourced from all over India. Despite his success, Rakesh faced a dilemma—how to price his spices in a way that would attract customers, cover his costs, and maximize his profits.

One evening, after a long day at the market, Rakesh's friend Anjali, who ran a profitable online store, visited him. "Rakesh," she said, "You have the best spices in town, but your pricing seems inconsistent. Some customers think your prices are too high, while others are surprised at how cheap some items are. Have you thought about adopting a strategic approach to pricing?"

Rakesh, eager to improve his business, replied, "I know pricing is important, but I'm not sure how to set prices that balance all these factors. Can you help me understand how to make smart pricing decisions?"

Anjali smiled and agreed to guide Rakesh through the complexities of pricing decisions, a journey that would help him find the perfect balance between value, cost, and customer expectations.

11.1 What Are Pricing Decisions?

Rakesh's First Lesson:

Rakesh learned that **pricing decisions** are a critical aspect of a company's overall strategy. Pricing affects how customers perceive a product, impacts sales and profitability, and influences the competitive positioning of the product in the market. Setting the right price requires a careful balance of multiple factors, including costs, competition, customer demand, and perceived value.

Meaning of Pricing Decisions:

Pricing decisions refer to the process of determining the appropriate price for a product or service. This involves considering factors such as production costs, market conditions, competitor pricing, and the target audience's willingness to pay. Effective pricing strategies can maximize profitability, enhance market share, and establish a strong brand positioning.

Famous Definitions of Pricing:

1. **Philip Kotler:***"Price is the amount of money charged for a product or service, or the sum of the values that customers exchange for the benefits of having or using the product or service."*
2. **Significance:** Kotler's definition highlights the idea that pricing is not just about the monetary cost, but also about the value that customers perceive in the product or service.
3. **Edmund Jerome McCarthy:***"Pricing is the marketing function that adjusts the cost of products or services to the economic environment and the psychological climate of the marketplace."*
4. **Significance:** McCarthy emphasizes that pricing is influenced by both economic factors and customer psychology, requiring marketers to consider both when setting prices.

Importance of Pricing Decisions:

1. **Profitability:**

- Pricing directly affects a company's profitability. Setting the right price can ensure that the business covers its costs and generates a healthy profit margin.
- **Example:** Rakesh needed to ensure that his prices covered the cost of sourcing high-quality spices and left enough margin for profit.

2. **Market Positioning:**

    - The price of a product helps position it in the market, signaling to customers whether it is a premium offering or a budget-friendly option.
    - **Example:** Rakesh wanted his premium saffron to be perceived as a luxury item, so he needed to price it higher than other spices.

3. **Customer Perception:**

    - Customers often associate price with quality. A well-thought-out pricing strategy can influence how customers perceive the value of a product.
    - **Example:** If Rakesh priced his top-quality spices too low, customers might question their authenticity or quality.

4. **Competitive Advantage:**

    - Strategic pricing can provide a competitive edge, allowing a company to attract customers away from competitors.
    - **Example:** Rakesh considered offering discounts on bulk purchases to attract customers who might otherwise buy from his competitors.

11.2 Factors Influencing Pricing Decisions

As Rakesh delved deeper into pricing strategies, he realized that several key factors must be considered when making pricing decisions.

1. Cost-Based Pricing:

Cost-based pricing involves setting prices based on the cost of producing the product, plus a markup for profit. This method ensures that all costs are covered and that the business remains profitable.

- **Types of Costs:**

    - **Fixed Costs:** Costs that remain constant regardless of the level of production, such as rent and salaries.
    - **Variable Costs:** Costs that vary with production levels, such as raw materials and packaging.
    - **Total Cost:** The sum of fixed and variable costs.
    - **Example:** Rakesh calculated the total cost of sourcing, packaging, and distributing his spices to determine the minimum price he needed to charge to break even.

2. Customer Value-Based Pricing:

Customer value-based pricing sets prices based on the perceived value of the product to the customer rather than the cost of production. This approach considers what customers are willing to pay based on the benefits they perceive.

- **Perceived Value:** The customer's assessment of the product's worth, considering its quality, features, brand reputation, and the alternatives available.
- **Example:** Rakesh knew that his customers valued the authenticity and freshness of his spices, so he priced them higher than competitors' offerings, reflecting their premium nature.

3. Competition-Based Pricing:

Competition-based pricing involves setting prices based on what competitors are charging for similar products. This strategy is often used in highly competitive markets.

- **Price Matching:** Setting prices similar to competitors to remain competitive.
- **Price Undercutting:** Setting lower prices to attract price-sensitive customers.
- **Premium Pricing:** Setting higher prices to differentiate the product as superior.
- **Example:** Rakesh analyzed the pricing of other spice vendors in the market and decided to position his products slightly higher to emphasize their premium quality.

4. Market Demand:

Market demand plays a crucial role in pricing decisions. Higher demand can allow for higher prices, while lower demand may require price reductions to stimulate sales.

- **Elasticity of Demand:**The degree to which the quantity demanded of a product changes in response to a change in price.
    - **Inelastic Demand:** Price changes have little effect on demand.
    - **Elastic Demand:** Price changes significantly affect demand.
- **Example:** Rakesh noticed that demand for his unique spice blends was relatively inelastic, allowing him to maintain higher prices without losing customers.

5. Economic Conditions:

Economic factors such as inflation, recession, and changes in consumer purchasing power can influence pricing decisions. Businesses may need to adjust prices in response to economic shifts.

- **Example:** During an economic downturn, Rakesh considered offering smaller, more affordable packages of his premium spices to cater to budget-conscious customers.

6. Legal and Ethical Considerations:

Legal regulations, such as price controls, minimum wage laws, and anti-price gouging laws, must be considered when setting prices. Ethical considerations also play a role, ensuring that pricing is fair and transparent.

- **Example:** Rakesh ensured that his pricing complied with local regulations and avoided unethical practices such as price discrimination or misleading pricing tactics.

11.3 Pricing Strategies

Rakesh learned that there are various pricing strategies that businesses can adopt, depending on their goals, market conditions, and customer segments.

1. Penetration Pricing:

Penetration pricing involves setting a low price to enter a competitive market and attract customers quickly. This strategy is often used for new products to gain market share.

- **Example:** To introduce a new range of masala blends, Rakesh considered using penetration pricing to attract customers who were not familiar with his brand.

2. Skimming Pricing:

Skimming pricing involves setting a high initial price for a new or innovative product, targeting customers who are willing to pay a premium. The price is gradually lowered over time as competition increases.

- **Example:** Rakesh introduced a limited-edition saffron blend at a high price, targeting gourmet chefs and food enthusiasts. Once the initial demand was satisfied, he lowered the price to appeal to a broader audience.

3. Psychological Pricing:

Psychological pricing uses pricing tactics that influence customer perception and behavior, such as setting prices slightly below a round number (e.g., ₹999 instead of ₹1000).

- **Example:** Rakesh priced his popular garam masala at ₹199 per pack, making it seem more affordable to customers than a price of ₹200.

4. Premium Pricing:

Premium pricing involves setting a high price to reflect the superior quality, exclusivity, or luxury status of a product. This strategy is often used for premium or luxury brands.

- **Example:** Rakesh maintained premium pricing for his handpicked, organic spices, emphasizing their rarity and high quality.

5. Value-Based Pricing:

Value-based pricing sets prices based on the perceived value to the customer, rather than on the cost of production. This strategy requires a deep understanding of the customer's needs and how much they are willing to pay for the benefits the product provides.

- **Example:** Rakesh priced his spice blends based on the unique flavors and health benefits they offered, which customers valued highly.

6. Cost-Plus Pricing:

Cost-plus pricing involves adding a standard markup to the cost of producing the product. This method ensures that all costs are covered and a profit margin is achieved.

- **Example:** Rakesh used cost-plus pricing for his basic spice offerings, adding a 20% markup to cover costs and ensure profitability.

7. Bundle Pricing:

Bundle pricing offers multiple products or services together at a lower price than if purchased separately. This strategy encourages customers to buy more and increases overall sales.

- **Example:** Rakesh offered a "Spice Starter Kit" that included a variety of his most popular spices at a bundled price, appealing to customers looking to stock their kitchen with essentials.

8. Dynamic Pricing:

Dynamic pricing involves adjusting prices in real-time based on demand, competition, and other external factors. This strategy is common in industries like travel, hospitality, and e-commerce.

- **Example:** Rakesh considered using dynamic pricing for his online store, adjusting prices based on demand during peak shopping seasons.

9. Discount and Promotional Pricing:

Discount and promotional pricing involve temporarily reducing prices to boost sales, clear inventory, or attract customers. This strategy is often used during sales events or to introduce new products.

- **Example:** During the festive season, Rakesh offered discounts on bulk purchases of his spices, attracting customers looking to prepare large meals for celebrations.

11.4 The Role of Price Elasticity in Pricing Decisions

Rakesh discovered that understanding price elasticity is crucial for making informed pricing decisions. **Price elasticity of demand** measures how sensitive the quantity demanded of a product is to changes in its price.

1. Elastic Demand:

When demand is elastic, a small change in price leads to a significant change in the quantity demanded. In such cases, businesses need to be cautious with price increases, as they can lead to a sharp decline in sales.

- **Example:** Rakesh noticed that sales of his entry-level spice blends were highly elastic, meaning that even a small price increase could result in a significant drop in demand.

2. Inelastic Demand:

When demand is inelastic, changes in price have little effect on the quantity demanded. Products with inelastic demand can often sustain higher prices without losing customers.

- **Example:** Rakesh's premium saffron, which had few substitutes and was highly valued by customers, exhibited inelastic demand, allowing him to maintain higher prices without affecting sales.

3. Factors Affecting Price Elasticity:

- **Availability of Substitutes:** Products with many substitutes tend to have more elastic demand.
- **Necessity vs. Luxury:** Necessities typically have inelastic demand, while luxury items have more elastic demand.
- **Customer Loyalty:** Strong brand loyalty can make demand more inelastic.
- **Example:** Rakesh's loyal customer base for his unique spice blends made demand less sensitive to price changes, allowing for greater pricing flexibility.

11.5 Practical Activity: Developing a Pricing Strategy

Activity Name: The Price is Right

- **Setup:** Students will be divided into groups, and each group will choose a product (real or fictional). They will develop a pricing strategy based on the product's costs, market demand, competition, and perceived value.

- **Task:** Groups will present their pricing strategy to the class, explaining how they arrived at their chosen price and how it aligns with their overall marketing and business objectives. They will also discuss potential challenges and how they plan to address them.
- **Presentation:** Each group will showcase their pricing decisions, including any psychological pricing tactics, discount strategies, or dynamic pricing models they plan to use, followed by a class discussion on the effectiveness of their strategies.

11.6 The Art of Pricing

As Rakesh wrapped up his lessons on pricing decisions, he understood that pricing is both an art and a science. It requires a deep understanding of costs, customer behavior, competition, and market conditions. By carefully considering these factors and choosing the right pricing strategy, Rakesh was able to set prices that attracted customers, covered his costs, and maximized his profits.

With his newfound knowledge, Rakesh confidently adjusted the pricing for Spice World's products, ensuring that each spice was priced to reflect its value, appeal to the target market, and maintain a competitive edge. He realized that pricing was not just about numbers—it was about understanding his customers, his market, and his business, and finding the perfect balance between them all.

CHAPTER XIII

Distribution Channels – The Pathway to Market Success

The Journey of the Handcrafted Goods

In the picturesque town of Jaipur, renowned for its vibrant culture and traditional crafts, there was an artisan named Kavita who created beautiful, handcrafted textiles. Kavita's business, "Threads of Jaipur," was a small but growing venture. Despite the demand for her unique products, she faced a significant challenge—getting her textiles to customers across India and beyond.

One day, her friend Vikram, a successful entrepreneur in the logistics industry, visited her workshop. "Kavita," Vikram said, "Your textiles are exceptional, but to grow your business, you need to think beyond making beautiful products. You must find the right ways to get them into the hands of customers far and wide."

Kavita replied, "I know distribution is important, but I'm unsure how to reach more customers effectively. Can you help me understand how to set up and manage distribution channels?"

Vikram smiled and agreed to guide Kavita through the complexities of distribution channels, a journey that would help her connect her handcrafted goods with customers around the world.

12.1 What Are Distribution Channels?

Kavita's First Lesson:

Kavita learned that **distribution channels** are the pathways through which products travel from the manufacturer to the end consumer. These channels include intermediaries such as wholesalers, retailers, and distributors, as well as logistics elements like warehousing and transportation. Effective distribution is essential for ensuring that products reach the right customers at the right time and in the right condition.

Meaning of Distribution Channels:

Distribution channels refer to the network of intermediaries or outlets that a business uses to distribute its products or services to customers. These channels can be direct, involving direct sales to customers, or indirect, involving intermediaries such as wholesalers and retailers.

Famous Definitions of Distribution Channels:

1. **Philip Kotler:** *"A distribution channel is a set of interdependent organizations involved in the process of making a product or service available for use or consumption by the consumer or business user."*
2. **Significance:** Kotler's definition emphasizes the interdependence of different organizations in the distribution process, highlighting the importance of collaboration and coordination.
3. **Cundiff and Still:** *"A marketing channel is the structure of intra-company organization units and extra-company agents and dealers, wholesale and retail, through which a commodity, product, or service is marketed."*
4. **Significance:** This definition highlights the involvement of both internal and external entities in the distribution process, reflecting the complexity of modern distribution networks.

Importance of Distribution Channels:

1. **Market Reach:**

- Distribution channels allow businesses to expand their market reach by making products available to a broader audience, both locally and globally.
- **Example:** Kavita realized that by partnering with retailers and wholesalers, she could reach customers in cities where she didn't have a physical presence.

2. **Customer Convenience:**

    - Effective distribution channels ensure that products are available to customers when and where they want them, enhancing customer satisfaction and loyalty.
    - **Example:** By offering her textiles through both online platforms and physical stores, Kavita made it convenient for customers to purchase her products.

3. **Efficient Supply Chain Management:**

    - Well-managed distribution channels contribute to an efficient supply chain, reducing costs and improving delivery times.
    - **Example:** Kavita partnered with a reliable warehousing service to store her textiles closer to major markets, reducing delivery times and costs.

4. **Competitive Advantage:**

    - A strong distribution network can provide a competitive advantage by ensuring product availability and enabling faster delivery than competitors.
    - **Example:** Kavita's efficient distribution network allowed her to offer faster delivery times than her competitors, making her products more attractive to customers.

12.2 Types of Distribution Channels

As Kavita delved deeper into distribution strategies, she learned that there are different types of distribution channels, each suited to different types of products, markets, and business goals.

1. Direct Distribution Channels:

Direct distribution channels involve selling products directly to the end consumer without intermediaries. This can be done through physical stores, online platforms, or direct sales teams.

- **Advantages:**

    - Greater control over the customer experience.
    - Higher profit margins by eliminating intermediaries.
    - Direct feedback from customers, allowing for quicker adjustments.
    - **Example:** Kavita set up an online store to sell her textiles directly to customers, allowing her to control the branding and customer service experience.

- **Challenges:**

    - Requires significant investment in marketing and distribution infrastructure.
    - Managing logistics and customer service can be complex.

2. Indirect Distribution Channels:
Indirect distribution channels involve intermediaries, such as wholesalers, retailers, or agents, who help distribute the product to the end consumer. This approach is common for businesses that want to reach a larger audience without handling all aspects of distribution themselves.

- **Advantages:**
  - Wider market reach through established networks of intermediaries.
  - Lower distribution costs by leveraging the infrastructure of intermediaries.
  - Focus on core business activities, such as production and marketing.
  - **Example:** Kavita partnered with a chain of retail stores to sell her textiles, reaching customers in different regions without having to set up her own stores.
- **Challenges:**
  - Less control over how the product is marketed and sold.
  - Profit margins are reduced due to intermediary fees.

3. Dual Distribution Channels:
Dual distribution involves using both direct and indirect channels to reach customers. This approach allows businesses to maximize their market coverage by catering to different customer preferences.

- **Advantages:**
  - Increased market reach and customer accessibility.
  - Flexibility in distribution, catering to different segments through different channels.
  - **Example:** Kavita used dual distribution by selling her textiles both online (direct) and through retail stores (indirect), reaching a wider audience.
- **Challenges:**
  - Potential for channel conflict, where direct sales may compete with indirect channels.
  - Requires careful coordination to ensure consistent branding and customer experience.

4. Multi-Channel Distribution:
Multi-channel distribution involves using multiple channels simultaneously to reach customers. This can include a mix of physical stores, online platforms, catalogs, and direct sales.

- **Advantages:**
  - Greater customer reach and convenience.
  - Diversified revenue streams, reducing dependence on a single channel.
  - **Example:** Kavita expanded her distribution strategy by selling through her online store, retail partners, and a catalog, allowing customers to purchase through their preferred method.
- **Challenges:**

- Requires careful management to avoid channel conflicts and ensure consistent pricing and customer experience across channels.

5. Omnichannel Distribution:

Omnichannel distribution is a seamless integration of multiple channels, providing customers with a unified shopping experience regardless of how they interact with the brand. This approach ensures that customers have a consistent experience whether they shop online, in-store, or through other channels.

- **Advantages:**
  - Enhanced customer experience through seamless integration of channels.
  - Increased customer loyalty by offering convenience and flexibility.
  - **Example:** Kavita implemented an omnichannel strategy where customers could browse her textiles online, purchase them in-store, and return or exchange items through any channel.
- **Challenges:**
  - Complex and costly to implement, requiring significant investment in technology and logistics.
  - Requires consistent branding, pricing, and customer service across all channels.

12.3 Retailing: The Final Link to the Consumer

Kavita learned that **retailing** is a crucial part of the distribution process, as it represents the final link between the product and the consumer. Retailers play a key role in providing products to customers, offering a variety of purchasing options, and creating an environment where customers can interact with the brand.

1. Types of Retailers:

Retailers come in various forms, each serving different customer needs and offering different experiences.

- **Department Stores:**
  - Large stores offering a wide range of products across different categories, often with a focus on customer service.
  - **Example:** Kavita considered selling her textiles through a premium department store known for its curated selection of high-quality products.
- **Specialty Stores:**
  - Retailers that focus on a specific category or niche, offering a deep assortment of products within that category.
  - **Example:** Kavita partnered with a specialty store that focused on handcrafted goods and artisan products, aligning with her brand's identity.
- **Supermarkets and Hypermarkets:**
  - Large retail outlets that offer a wide range of products, including groceries, household items, and clothing, often at competitive prices.

- **Example:** While Kavita's textiles were not a typical supermarket item, she explored opportunities to offer smaller, everyday items like scarves and handkerchiefs through such outlets.

- **Convenience Stores:**
  - Small, neighborhood stores offering a limited range of products, typically focused on convenience and quick purchases.
  - **Example:** Kavita's products, which are premium and handcrafted, were less suited to convenience stores, but she explored the idea of offering select items in upscale urban convenience stores.

- **E-commerce:**
  - Online retailing, where products are sold through websites or online marketplaces, offering convenience and a wide reach.
  - **Example:** Kavita's online store became a significant part of her retail strategy, allowing her to reach customers worldwide.

- **Pop-up Shops:**
  - Temporary retail spaces that allow brands to create a unique, short-term retail experience.
  - **Example:** Kavita used pop-up shops during festivals and special events to showcase her textiles and attract new customers.

2. The Role of Retailers:
Retailers play several key roles in the distribution process, including:

- **Providing Customer Access:**
  - Retailers make products accessible to customers by offering them in locations where they shop regularly.
  - **Example:** By partnering with well-known retail stores, Kavita made her textiles easily accessible to customers across different regions.

- **Creating a Shopping Experience:**
  - Retailers create an environment that enhances the shopping experience, influencing how customers perceive the brand.
  - **Example:** Kavita worked with her retail partners to ensure that her textiles were displayed in a way that reflected their premium nature, creating a luxurious shopping experience.

- **Offering Additional Services:**
  - Retailers often provide additional services such as product demonstrations, customer support, and return/exchange policies.
  - **Example:** Kavita ensured that her retail partners offered personalized service, such as helping customers choose the right textiles for their needs and offering customization options.

12.4 Wholesaling: The Backbone of Distribution

As Kavita expanded her business, she realized that **wholesaling** played a critical role in her distribution strategy. Wholesalers act as intermediaries between manufacturers and retailers, buying products in bulk and selling them in smaller quantities to retailers or other businesses.

1. Types of Wholesalers:

Wholesalers can be classified into several categories based on their functions and the types of products they handle.

- **Merchant Wholesalers:**
  - Independently owned businesses that buy products in bulk from manufacturers and sell them to retailers or other wholesalers. They take ownership of the goods and are responsible for storage and distribution.
  - **Example:** Kavita partnered with a merchant wholesaler who specialized in handcrafted goods, helping her distribute her textiles to retailers across the country.
- **Agents and Brokers:**
  - Intermediaries who do not take ownership of the goods but facilitate sales between manufacturers and buyers. They earn a commission on sales.
  - **Example:** Kavita used an agent to connect with international retailers, allowing her to enter new markets without taking on the complexities of direct distribution.
- **Drop Shippers:**
  - Wholesalers who do not handle or store the goods. Instead, they take orders and have the manufacturer ship the products directly to the buyer.
  - **Example:** For her online store, Kavita considered using a drop shipper to fulfill large orders, reducing the need for her to manage inventory and shipping.
- **Rack Jobbers:**
  - Wholesalers who manage inventory for retailers by placing and maintaining products on racks in stores, particularly in grocery stores and drugstores.
  - **Example:** Although not directly applicable to her textiles, Kavita learned about rack jobbers as an option for smaller accessories or related products that could be placed in stores.

2. Functions of Wholesalers:

Wholesalers provide several key functions that support manufacturers and retailers:

- **Bulk Breaking:**
  - Wholesalers buy in bulk and sell in smaller quantities, making it easier for retailers to manage inventory.
  - **Example:** Kavita's wholesaler bought large quantities of her textiles, breaking them down into smaller shipments for distribution to various retail stores.
- **Warehousing:**

   - Wholesalers store products in their warehouses, reducing the storage burden on manufacturers and retailers.
   - **Example:** Kavita's wholesaler provided warehousing services, ensuring that her textiles were stored safely and ready for quick distribution.

- **Transportation:**

   - Wholesalers often handle the transportation of goods from manufacturers to retailers, ensuring timely delivery.
   - **Example:** Kavita relied on her wholesaler to manage the logistics of transporting her textiles to different regions, allowing her to focus on production.

- **Financing:**

   - Wholesalers may offer credit to retailers, allowing them to purchase products and pay later, which helps retailers manage their cash flow.
   - **Example:** Kavita's wholesaler offered flexible payment terms to retailers, making it easier for them to stock her textiles without immediate payment.

- **Market Information:**

   - Wholesalers provide manufacturers with valuable market information, such as trends, customer preferences, and competitor activity.
   - **Example:** Kavita received regular updates from her wholesaler about which of her products were selling well and what trends were emerging in the market.

12.5 Warehousing and Physical Distribution

Kavita learned that effective **warehousing** and **physical distribution** are crucial for ensuring that products are stored safely and delivered efficiently to customers.

1. Warehousing:

Warehousing involves the storage of goods until they are needed for distribution. Effective warehousing ensures that products are available when and where they are needed, minimizing delays and stockouts.

- **Types of Warehouses:**

   - **Private Warehouses:** Owned and operated by a company for its own use.
   - **Public Warehouses:** Operated by third parties, offering storage services to multiple businesses.
   - **Distribution Centers:** Specialized warehouses designed for quick turnover of goods, focusing on the rapid movement of products through the supply chain.
   - **Example:** Kavita used a public warehouse near a major distribution hub, allowing her textiles to be stored close to her key markets.

2. Functions of Warehousing:

Warehousing provides several essential functions that support the overall distribution strategy:

- **Storage:** Warehouses provide safe storage for products until they are needed for distribution.

- **Inventory Management:** Warehouses help businesses manage inventory levels, ensuring that products are available when needed and reducing the risk of stockouts.
- **Order Fulfillment:** Warehouses play a key role in order fulfillment, picking and packing products for shipment to customers or retailers.
- **Example:** Kavita's warehouse handled inventory management and order fulfillment for her online store, ensuring that orders were processed quickly and accurately.

3. Physical Distribution:

Physical distribution, also known as logistics, involves the movement of goods from the manufacturer to the end consumer. Effective physical distribution ensures that products are delivered in a timely, cost-effective manner.

- **Key Components of Physical Distribution:**

  - **Transportation:** Choosing the right mode of transportation (e.g., road, rail, air, sea) to balance cost, speed, and reliability.
  - **Inventory Control:** Managing inventory levels to meet customer demand without overstocking.
  - **Order Processing:** Efficiently processing orders to ensure accurate and timely delivery.
  - **Example:** Kavita used a combination of road and air transportation to deliver her textiles to different regions, balancing cost and speed depending on the destination.

- **Challenges in Physical Distribution:**

  - **Cost Management:** Keeping distribution costs under control while maintaining service levels.
  - **Speed vs. Cost:** Balancing the need for fast delivery with the cost implications of different transportation modes.
  - **Coordination:** Ensuring smooth coordination between different elements of the distribution network, such as warehouses, transportation providers, and retailers.
  - **Example:** Kavita worked with a logistics partner to optimize her distribution routes, reducing costs while maintaining timely delivery.

12.6 Practical Activity: Designing a Distribution Strategy

Activity Name: The Path to Market

- **Setup:** Students will be divided into groups, and each group will create a distribution strategy for a fictional product. They will decide on the type of distribution channels to use, the role of retailers and wholesalers, and the warehousing and logistics requirements.
- **Task:** Groups will present their distribution strategy to the class, explaining how they plan to reach their target customers efficiently and effectively. They will also discuss the challenges they might face and how they plan to overcome them.
- **Presentation:** Each group will showcase their distribution plan, including channel selection, retail partnerships, wholesaling strategies, warehousing, and logistics, followed by a class discussion on the effectiveness and feasibility of their strategies.

12.7 Building the Pathway to Success

As Kavita completed her journey through distribution channels, she realized that creating a successful product is only part of the challenge. Ensuring that the product reaches the right customers, at the right time, and in the right condition is equally important. By understanding and managing her distribution channels effectively, Kavita was able to expand her market reach, improve customer satisfaction, and grow her business.

With the guidance of Vikram and her newfound knowledge, Kavita built a distribution network that connected her handcrafted textiles with customers across India and beyond. She understood that the success of her business depended not just on the quality of her products, but on the efficiency and effectiveness of the entire distribution process. As her business grew, Kavita remained committed to finding new and innovative ways to reach her customers, ensuring that Threads of Jaipur continued to thrive in a competitive market.

CHAPTER XIV

Conceptual Introduction to Supply Chain Management – Connecting the Dots

The Flow of the Perfect Cup of Tea

In the serene hills of Darjeeling, known for producing some of the world's finest tea, there was a small tea estate owned by Arjun. His estate, "Golden Hills," was famous for its exquisite, handpicked tea leaves that were loved by connoisseurs across the globe. However, as demand for his tea grew, Arjun faced a new challenge—how to ensure that every cup of tea, whether enjoyed in Kolkata or London, delivered the same freshness and flavor as when it was first picked.

One day, while discussing the complexities of his business with his friend Priya, a logistics expert, Arjun expressed his concerns. "Priya," he said, "I understand how to grow and harvest the best tea, but getting it to my customers without losing quality is a different story. How do I manage all these moving parts effectively?"

Priya smiled and replied, "What you're talking about is supply chain management. It's about making sure that everything, from the moment the tea leaves are picked to the moment they're brewed, works together seamlessly. Let me guide you through the basics of how it all connects."

With Priya's help, Arjun embarked on a journey to understand the concepts of Supply Chain Management (SCM), which would help him maintain the quality and integrity of his tea as it traveled from his estate to tea cups around the world.

13.1 What is Supply Chain Management (SCM)?

Arjun's First Lesson:

Arjun learned that **Supply Chain Management (SCM)** is the coordination and management of all activities involved in sourcing, procurement, production, and logistics, with the ultimate goal of delivering a product to the end consumer efficiently and effectively. SCM is about creating a seamless flow of goods, information, and finances from suppliers to manufacturers to distributors to retailers, and finally, to the customer.

Meaning of Supply Chain Management:

Supply Chain Management (SCM) refers to the integrated management of the flow of goods, services, and information from the initial stages of raw material procurement to the final delivery of the finished product to the consumer. SCM involves the planning, execution, and control of supply chain activities with the aim of creating value, building a competitive infrastructure, leveraging logistics, synchronizing supply with demand, and measuring performance globally.

Famous Definitions of Supply Chain Management:

1. **Martin Christopher:***"Supply Chain Management is the management of upstream and downstream relationships with suppliers and customers to deliver superior customer value at less cost to the supply chain as a whole."*
2. **Significance:** Christopher's definition emphasizes the importance of managing relationships across the entire supply chain to enhance value and reduce costs.
3. **Institute of Supply Management (ISM):***"Supply Chain Management encompasses the planning and management of all activities involved in sourcing, procurement, conversion, and logistics management. It also includes coordination and collaboration with channel partners, which can be suppliers, intermediaries, third-party service providers, and customers."*
4. **Significance:** This definition highlights the comprehensive nature of SCM, including the need for collaboration and coordination among various supply chain partners.

Importance of Supply Chain Management:

1. **Enhanced Efficiency:**
    - SCM helps streamline operations by ensuring that each part of the supply chain works in harmony, reducing waste and inefficiencies.
    - **Example:** Arjun learned that by optimizing the timing of when his tea leaves were picked, processed, and shipped, he could reduce spoilage and ensure that customers received the freshest possible product.
2. **Cost Reduction:**
    - Effective SCM reduces costs by improving the flow of goods and information, minimizing delays, and reducing the need for excess inventory.
    - **Example:** By better coordinating with his suppliers and logistics partners, Arjun was able to lower his transportation costs and reduce the need for costly warehousing.
3. **Improved Customer Satisfaction:**
    - A well-managed supply chain ensures that products are delivered on time, in the right quantity, and in perfect condition, enhancing customer satisfaction.
    - **Example:** Arjun's customers appreciated the consistent quality of his tea, which arrived fresh and on time, thanks to his improved supply chain management.
4. **Competitive Advantage:**
    - Companies with strong SCM capabilities can respond more quickly to market changes, customer demands, and supply chain disruptions, giving them a competitive edge.
    - **Example:** Arjun's ability to quickly fulfill large orders during peak seasons gave him an advantage over competitors who struggled with delays.
5. **Global Reach:**
    - SCM enables businesses to operate on a global scale, sourcing materials from different parts of the world and selling products in international markets.
    - **Example:** Arjun expanded his market by exporting his tea to Europe and North America, using SCM strategies to navigate the complexities of international logistics.

13.2 Components of the Supply Chain

Priya explained to Arjun that the supply chain is made up of several key components, each playing a crucial role in ensuring the smooth flow of goods from the source to the consumer.

1. Sourcing and Procurement:

Sourcing and procurement involve the process of finding and acquiring the raw materials, components, and services needed to produce a product. This component focuses on selecting suppliers, negotiating contracts, and managing relationships with vendors.

- **Example:** Arjun sourced the best tea plants from trusted nurseries and procured the necessary tools and materials for harvesting and processing the tea leaves.

2. Production and Manufacturing:

Production and manufacturing are the processes by which raw materials are transformed into finished products. This component involves planning, scheduling, and managing the production process to ensure efficiency and quality.

- **Example:** Arjun's tea leaves were carefully processed, dried, and packaged on-site at his estate, ensuring that the delicate flavors were preserved.

3. Inventory Management:

Inventory management involves overseeing the storage, handling, and control of products at various stages of the supply chain. Effective inventory management ensures that the right amount of product is available when needed, without overstocking or stockouts.

- **Example:** Arjun maintained a balanced inventory of processed tea, ensuring that he could meet customer demand without overproducing or running out of stock.

4. Warehousing:

Warehousing involves the storage of goods at various points in the supply chain. Warehouses serve as distribution hubs, where products are stored until they are needed for further processing or delivery.

- **Example:** Arjun used a climate-controlled warehouse to store his tea, preserving its freshness until it was ready to be shipped to customers.

5. Logistics and Transportation:

Logistics and transportation involve the movement of goods from one location to another, including the management of shipping routes, modes of transport, and delivery schedules. This component is critical for ensuring timely and cost-effective delivery of products.

- **Example:** Arjun coordinated with logistics providers to transport his tea from Darjeeling to various markets around the world, choosing the fastest and most reliable routes.

6. Distribution and Retail:

Distribution and retail involve the final stages of the supply chain, where products are delivered to retailers or directly to consumers. This component includes managing relationships with distributors, retailers, and e-commerce platforms.

- **Example:** Arjun's tea was sold through a network of specialty tea shops, online platforms, and gourmet food stores, reaching customers both locally and internationally.

7. Information Flow and Technology:

The flow of information is critical in SCM, as it enables the coordination of activities across the supply chain. Technology plays a key role in managing information, providing real-time visibility into inventory levels, production schedules, and transportation status.

- **Example:** Arjun used supply chain management software to track the movement of his tea leaves from the estate to the customer, ensuring that every step of the process was monitored and managed efficiently.

8. Returns Management:

Returns management, also known as reverse logistics, involves handling returned products, managing repairs or replacements, and processing refunds. Effective returns management is important for maintaining customer satisfaction and minimizing losses.

- **Example:** Arjun had a system in place to manage any returns or complaints, ensuring that customers who were dissatisfied with their purchase could receive a replacement or refund promptly.

13.3 Key Concepts in Supply Chain Management

As Arjun deepened his understanding of SCM, Priya introduced him to several key concepts that are essential for managing a supply chain effectively.

1. Supply Chain Integration:

Supply chain integration refers to the alignment and coordination of activities across the entire supply chain, from suppliers to manufacturers to distributors to retailers. Integration ensures that all parts of the supply chain work together seamlessly, reducing inefficiencies and improving overall performance.

- **Example:** Arjun worked closely with his suppliers and logistics partners to ensure that every part of his supply chain was aligned with his goals of quality and efficiency.

2. Demand Forecasting:

Demand forecasting involves predicting future customer demand based on historical data, market trends, and other factors. Accurate demand forecasting is essential for managing inventory levels, production schedules, and distribution plans.

- **Example:** Arjun used demand forecasting to plan his production and inventory levels, ensuring that he could meet peak demand during the holiday season without overproducing.

3. Just-in-Time (JIT) Inventory:

Just-in-Time (JIT) inventory is a strategy that involves producing or ordering only what is needed, when it is needed, to reduce inventory costs and minimize waste. JIT requires precise coordination and reliable suppliers.

- **Example:** Arjun adopted a JIT approach to inventory management, reducing the amount of tea stored in his warehouse by producing and shipping only what was needed to fulfill orders.

4. Supply Chain Resilience:

Supply chain resilience refers to the ability of a supply chain to adapt to disruptions, such as natural disasters, supplier failures, or market fluctuations. Building a resilient supply chain involves diversifying suppliers, maintaining safety stock, and developing contingency plans.

- **Example:** Arjun diversified his supplier base and established backup logistics providers to ensure that his supply chain could withstand unexpected disruptions.

5. Sustainability in Supply Chain:

Sustainability in supply chain management involves reducing the environmental and social impact of supply chain activities. This includes sourcing sustainable materials, minimizing waste, and reducing carbon emissions in transportation.

- **Example:** Arjun implemented sustainable practices in his supply chain, such as using eco-friendly packaging and choosing transportation methods with lower carbon footprints.

6. Total Quality Management (TQM):

Total Quality Management (TQM) is an approach that emphasizes continuous improvement and customer satisfaction throughout the supply chain. TQM involves setting high-quality standards, regularly measuring performance, and making improvements as needed.

- **Example:** Arjun applied TQM principles to ensure that every batch of tea met the highest standards of quality, from harvesting to packaging to delivery.

13.4 Practical Activity: Mapping the Supply Chain

Activity Name: The Supply Chain Puzzle

- **Setup:** Students will be divided into groups, and each group will select a product (real or fictional). They will map out the entire supply chain for that product, from sourcing raw materials to delivering the finished product to the customer.
- **Task:** Groups will identify key components of the supply chain, such as sourcing, production, logistics, and distribution. They will also highlight potential challenges and propose strategies for managing those challenges.
- **Presentation:** Each group will present their supply chain map to the class, explaining how they would manage each component and ensure that the product reaches the customer efficiently and effectively. The presentation will be followed by a class discussion on the strengths and weaknesses of each supply chain strategy.

13.5 The Flow of Success

As Arjun completed his journey through Supply Chain Management, he realized that SCM is much more than just moving products from one place to another. It's about creating a network of interconnected activities that work together to deliver value to the customer. By understanding and managing each component of his supply chain, Arjun was able to ensure that every cup of Golden Hills tea, whether enjoyed in a cozy café in Paris or a bustling market in Delhi, delivered the same exquisite taste and quality.

With Priya's guidance and his newfound knowledge of SCM, Arjun built a supply chain that was efficient, resilient, and sustainable. He understood that the success of his tea estate depended not only on the quality of the tea leaves but also on the effectiveness of the entire supply chain that brought those leaves to the world. As he looked forward to expanding his business, Arjun remained committed to continuously improving his supply chain, ensuring that Golden Hills tea continued to delight customers across the globe.

CHAPTER XV

Conceptual Introduction to Customer Relationship Marketing – Building Lasting Connections

The Tale of the Loyal Customer

In the bustling city of Mumbai, there was a small bookstore named "The Reader's Haven" run by Meera, a passionate lover of books. Her shop was more than just a place to buy books—it was a cozy retreat where readers could lose themselves in stories, share their love for literature, and connect with other like-minded individuals. Meera had built a loyal customer base over the years, but as online bookstores gained popularity, she noticed that some of her regulars were being lured away by discounts and convenience.

One evening, while chatting with one of her long-time customers, Raj, he mentioned how much he appreciated the personal touch and community feel of The Reader's Haven. "Meera," he said, "I can buy books anywhere, but what keeps me coming back here is the connection I feel with this place. It's not just about the books; it's about how you make us feel valued and part of a community."

This conversation sparked an idea in Meera's mind. She realized that the secret to retaining her customers lay not just in selling books, but in nurturing relationships. Determined to build stronger connections with her customers, Meera decided to learn more about Customer Relationship Marketing (CRM) and how it could help her business thrive in the age of digital commerce.

14.1 What is Customer Relationship Marketing (CRM)?

Meera's First Lesson:

Meera discovered that **Customer Relationship Marketing (CRM)** is a strategy focused on building and maintaining long-term relationships with customers rather than simply focusing on individual transactions. CRM emphasizes customer satisfaction, loyalty, and engagement, with the goal of creating strong, lasting connections that encourage repeat business and word-of-mouth referrals.

Meaning of Customer Relationship Marketing:

Customer Relationship Marketing (CRM) is a business strategy that prioritizes the development of strong relationships with customers by understanding their needs, providing personalized experiences, and fostering loyalty. CRM involves a range of practices and tools designed to manage interactions with customers, track customer data, and enhance the overall customer experience.

Famous Definitions of Customer Relationship Marketing:

1. **Philip Kotler:***"Customer Relationship Marketing is the process of creating, maintaining, and enhancing strong, value-laden relationships with customers and other stakeholders."*
2. **Significance:** Kotler's definition highlights the importance of creating value through relationships, not just transactions, and suggests that CRM involves all stakeholders, not just customers.
3. **Berry and Parasuraman:***"Customer Relationship Marketing is a business approach that focuses on establishing, maintaining, and enhancing relationships with customers and other stakeholders at a profit, so that the objectives of both parties are met."*
4. **Significance:** This definition emphasizes the mutual benefits of CRM for both the business and the customer, highlighting the importance of relationship-building for long-term success.

Importance of Customer Relationship Marketing:

1. **Increased Customer Loyalty:**
    - CRM strategies help build customer loyalty by creating positive experiences and fostering emotional connections with the brand.
    - **Example:** Meera implemented a loyalty program at The Reader's Haven, offering exclusive discounts and early access to new arrivals for regular customers, which strengthened their loyalty to her store.
2. **Higher Customer Retention:**
    - Retaining existing customers is more cost-effective than acquiring new ones. CRM helps businesses keep customers satisfied and engaged, reducing churn.
    - **Example:** By regularly engaging with her customers through personalized recommendations and newsletters, Meera was able to keep them coming back to her bookstore instead of switching to online retailers.
3. **Enhanced Customer Satisfaction:**
    - CRM ensures that customers receive personalized attention and services tailored to their needs, leading to higher satisfaction levels.
    - **Example:** Meera made it a point to remember her customers' favorite genres and authors, offering personalized recommendations that made each visit to The Reader's Haven special.
4. **Increased Sales and Profitability:**
    - Loyal customers are more likely to make repeat purchases and refer others, leading to increased sales and profitability over time.
    - **Example:** Meera noticed that her loyal customers not only spent more on books but also brought their friends and family to the store, boosting overall sales.
5. **Better Customer Insights:**
    - CRM tools help businesses gather and analyze customer data, providing insights into customer preferences, behaviors, and needs. This data can be used to refine marketing strategies and improve customer experiences.
    - **Example:** Meera used a simple CRM system to track her customers' purchase histories, helping her understand which books were popular and tailoring her inventory accordingly.

14.2 Components of Customer Relationship Marketing

Meera learned that CRM is composed of several key components, each contributing to the overall goal of building strong customer relationships.

1. Customer Data Management:

Customer data management involves collecting, storing, and analyzing customer information, such as contact details, purchase history, preferences, and interactions. This data is crucial for understanding customer needs and personalizing marketing efforts.

- **Example:** Meera kept detailed records of her customers' preferences and purchase history, allowing her to send personalized recommendations and offers.

2. Segmentation and Targeting:

Segmentation involves dividing the customer base into groups based on shared characteristics, such as demographics, buying behavior, or preferences. Targeting involves creating specific marketing strategies for each segment to address their unique needs and interests.

- **Example:** Meera segmented her customers into different groups, such as avid readers, casual buyers, and collectors, tailoring her marketing messages and offers to each group's preferences.

3. Personalization:

Personalization involves customizing the customer experience based on individual preferences and behaviors. This can include personalized marketing messages, product recommendations, and tailored offers.

- **Example:** Meera personalized her communications by addressing customers by name and recommending books based on their previous purchases, making each customer feel valued and understood.

4. Customer Engagement:

Customer engagement focuses on creating meaningful interactions with customers through various channels, such as email, social media, events, and in-store experiences. Engaged customers are more likely to be loyal and advocate for the brand.

- **Example:** Meera regularly hosted book readings and author events at her bookstore, creating opportunities for her customers to engage with the brand and each other.

5. Customer Service:

Customer service is a critical component of CRM, as it directly impacts customer satisfaction and loyalty. Providing excellent customer service ensures that customers' needs are met, problems are resolved quickly, and positive relationships are maintained.

- **Example:** Meera's attentive customer service, such as helping customers find specific books or placing special orders, made her bookstore a trusted and reliable place to shop.

6. Loyalty Programs:

Loyalty programs reward repeat customers for their continued business, encouraging them to keep coming back. These programs can include points systems, discounts, exclusive offers, and VIP experiences.

- **Example:** Meera's loyalty program offered points for every purchase, which customers could redeem for discounts or special gifts, incentivizing them to shop at The Reader's Haven more frequently.

7. Feedback and Continuous Improvement:

Gathering customer feedback is essential for understanding their experiences and identifying areas for improvement. Regularly seeking and acting on feedback helps businesses refine their CRM strategies and enhance customer satisfaction.

- **Example:** Meera encouraged her customers to share their thoughts on the bookstore's selection, service, and events, using their feedback to make improvements and better meet their needs.

14.3 Key Concepts in Customer Relationship Marketing

As Meera deepened her understanding of CRM, she discovered several key concepts that are fundamental to building strong customer relationships.

1. Customer Lifetime Value (CLV):

Customer Lifetime Value (CLV) is the total revenue a business can expect from a single customer over the duration of their relationship. Understanding CLV helps businesses prioritize long-term relationships and invest in customers who bring the most value.

- **Example:** Meera calculated the CLV of her most loyal customers, realizing that these individuals were worth investing in through personalized services and exclusive offers.

2. Customer Satisfaction:

Customer satisfaction is the degree to which a product or service meets or exceeds customer expectations. High customer satisfaction is a key driver of loyalty and positive word-of-mouth.

- **Example:** Meera focused on creating a welcoming atmosphere, offering knowledgeable recommendations, and providing exceptional service to ensure high levels of customer satisfaction.

3. Customer Retention:

Customer retention refers to the ability of a business to keep its customers over time. High retention rates indicate strong customer loyalty and effective CRM strategies.

- **Example:** Meera's focus on relationship-building and personalized service helped her retain a large percentage of her customers, even in the face of competition from online retailers.

4. Customer Advocacy:

Customer advocacy occurs when satisfied customers actively promote a brand to others, often through word-of-mouth or social media. Advocates are valuable assets, as they help attract new customers at little to no cost.

- **Example:** Many of Meera's customers became advocates for The Reader's Haven, recommending the bookstore to friends and sharing their positive experiences on social media.

5. Relationship Marketing:

Relationship marketing focuses on long-term customer engagement rather than short-term sales. It involves building trust, providing value, and nurturing relationships over time.

- **Example:** Meera adopted a relationship marketing approach by prioritizing customer connections, offering personalized experiences, and engaging with her community regularly.

6. Cross-Selling and Up-Selling:

Cross-selling involves offering additional products or services that complement the customer's initial purchase, while up-selling involves encouraging customers to purchase a more expensive or upgraded version of the product.

- **Example:** When a customer purchased a novel, Meera often recommended related books or limited-edition copies, increasing her sales through cross-selling and up-selling.

14.4 The Role of Technology in Customer Relationship Marketing

Meera realized that technology plays a crucial role in CRM by enabling businesses to collect, analyze, and act on customer data, as well as manage customer interactions across various channels.

1. Customer Relationship Management (CRM) Software:

CRM software is a tool that helps businesses manage customer data, track interactions, automate marketing efforts, and analyze customer behavior. It's essential for scaling CRM efforts and maintaining personalized relationships as the customer base grows.

- **Example:** Meera used a CRM system to store customer information, track purchase histories, and automate personalized email campaigns, helping her manage her growing customer base more effectively.

2. Data Analytics:

Data analytics involves analyzing customer data to identify trends, preferences, and behaviors. This information is used to refine marketing strategies, improve customer experiences, and predict future customer needs.

- **Example:** Meera used data analytics to identify which genres were most popular among her customers, allowing her to stock more of those books and offer targeted promotions.

3. Automation:

Automation tools enable businesses to streamline repetitive tasks, such as sending follow-up emails, managing loyalty programs, and processing orders. Automation ensures consistency and frees up time for more strategic CRM activities.

- **Example:** Meera automated her loyalty program, ensuring that customers received points and rewards automatically after each purchase, enhancing their experience without adding to her workload.

4. Social Media:

Social media platforms provide opportunities for businesses to engage with customers, build communities, and gather feedback. They also allow businesses to reach new audiences and encourage customer advocacy.

- **Example:** Meera used social media to connect with her customers, share updates about new arrivals, and host virtual book clubs, fostering a sense of community around The Reader's Haven.

5. Omnichannel CRM:

Omnichannel CRM involves managing customer interactions across multiple channels—such as in-store, online, email, and social media—while providing a seamless and consistent experience. It ensures that customers receive personalized attention no matter how they interact with the brand.

- **Example:** Meera's omnichannel CRM strategy allowed her to maintain consistent communication with her customers whether they visited the store, shopped online, or interacted with her on social media.

14.5 Practical Activity: Building a Customer Relationship Strategy

Activity Name: The Customer Connection

- **Setup:** Students will be divided into groups, and each group will create a CRM strategy for a fictional business. They will identify key customer segments, plan personalized marketing efforts, and design a loyalty program.
- **Task:** Groups will present their CRM strategy to the class, explaining how they plan to build and maintain strong customer relationships. They will also discuss the role of technology in implementing their strategy and how they will measure success.
- **Presentation:** Each group will showcase their CRM strategy, including customer segmentation, engagement tactics, and loyalty initiatives, followed by a class discussion on the effectiveness and feasibility of their plans.

14.6 Nurturing Lasting Relationships

As Meera embraced the principles of Customer Relationship Marketing, she realized that the key to her bookstore's success wasn't just in selling books, but in building lasting connections with her customers. By focusing on their needs, personalizing their experiences, and nurturing their loyalty, Meera was able to create a community of readers who valued The Reader's Haven as more than just a place to buy books.

With her newfound understanding of CRM, Meera implemented strategies that strengthened her relationships with existing customers and attracted new ones. She knew that in the competitive world of retail, it was these strong relationships that would set her apart and ensure the long-term success of her business. As The Reader's Haven continued to thrive, Meera remained committed to fostering the connections that made her bookstore a beloved destination for book lovers near and far.

CHAPTER XVI

The Promotion Mix – Crafting the Perfect Message

The Grand Launch of the New Coffee Blend

In the heart of Bangalore, known for its vibrant startup culture, there was a popular café called "Bean Bliss," owned by Arjun, a passionate coffee enthusiast. Arjun had just developed a new coffee blend, a unique fusion of local spices and premium coffee beans sourced from the Western Ghats. Excited about his creation, Arjun wanted to introduce it to the world in a way that would make a lasting impression.

One evening, as Arjun sat in his café, brainstorming ideas, his friend Kavita, a marketing expert, dropped by. "Arjun," she said, "You've created something special, but to make it a success, you need to promote it effectively. How do you plan to spread the word?"

Arjun sighed, "I've thought about putting up posters and maybe running a few ads online, but I'm not sure if that's enough. What else can I do to really get people excited about my new blend?"

Kavita smiled and replied, "Promoting your product is about more than just ads. It's about creating a mix of strategies that work together to reach your audience and persuade them to try your blend. Let me introduce you to the Promotion Mix and show you how to make your launch unforgettable."

And so began Arjun's journey into understanding the Promotion Mix and how it could help him craft the perfect message to launch his new coffee blend.

15.1 What is the Promotion Mix?

Arjun's First Lesson:

Arjun learned that the **Promotion Mix** is a combination of different promotional tools and strategies that a business uses to communicate with its target audience, promote its products, and persuade customers to make a purchase. The Promotion Mix includes personal selling, advertising, sales promotion, and publicity, each playing a unique role in creating a comprehensive promotional strategy.

Meaning of Promotion Mix:

The Promotion Mix refers to the blend of various promotional activities and tools that a company uses to achieve its marketing objectives. It involves selecting the right mix of personal selling, advertising, sales promotion, and publicity to effectively reach and engage the target audience, build brand awareness, and drive sales.

Famous Definitions of Promotion Mix:

1. **Philip Kotler:***"The promotion mix is the specific blend of advertising, personal selling, sales promotion, and public relations tools that the company uses to pursue its advertising and marketing objectives."*
2. **Significance:** Kotler's definition highlights the importance of blending different promotional tools to create a cohesive strategy that aligns with the company's overall marketing goals.
3. **Stanton, Etzel, and Walker:***"The promotion mix is the combination of promotional tools—including advertising, personal selling, sales promotion, and publicity—used by a firm to communicate with its audience and achieve its marketing objectives."*
4. **Significance:** This definition emphasizes the role of the promotion mix in communicating with the audience and achieving specific marketing objectives through a combination of tools.

Importance of the Promotion Mix:

1. **Effective Communication:**
    - The promotion mix ensures that businesses effectively communicate their product's value proposition to the target audience through various channels and tools.
    - **Example:** Arjun used a mix of advertising and publicity to create awareness about his new coffee blend, ensuring that his message reached a wide audience.
2. **Building Brand Awareness:**
    - A well-balanced promotion mix helps build brand awareness by consistently presenting the brand's message across different platforms.
    - **Example:** By using social media ads, in-store promotions, and public relations events, Arjun was able to increase awareness of Bean Bliss and its new coffee blend.
3. **Influencing Consumer Behavior:**
    - The promotion mix influences consumer behavior by providing information, creating desire, and motivating action through various promotional strategies.
    - **Example:** Arjun's sales promotions, such as limited-time discounts and free samples, encouraged customers to try the new blend, driving initial sales.
4. **Maximizing Reach:**
    - A diverse promotion mix allows businesses to reach a broader audience by leveraging different channels, each with its own strengths.
    - **Example:** Arjun's mix of online advertising, local events, and word-of-mouth publicity ensured that his message reached both tech-savvy coffee enthusiasts and traditional café-goers.
5. **Enhancing Customer Engagement:**
    - The promotion mix helps businesses engage with their customers by creating opportunities for interaction and feedback through personal selling, social media, and events.
    - **Example:** Arjun engaged with customers through in-store tastings and social media polls, gathering feedback on the new blend and building a stronger connection with his audience.

15.2 Components of the Promotion Mix

Kavita explained to Arjun that the Promotion Mix consists of four main components, each serving a distinct purpose in the overall promotional strategy.

1. Personal Selling:

Personal selling involves direct, face-to-face interaction between a sales representative and a potential customer. It is a personalized form of communication that allows businesses to address customer needs, answer questions, and persuade them to make a purchase.

- **Characteristics:**
    - High level of personal interaction.

- Customized communication based on customer needs.
- Opportunity for immediate feedback and negotiation.
- **Example:** Arjun trained his staff to engage with customers, offering detailed explanations about the origins and flavors of the new coffee blend, and answering any questions they had.

- **Advantages:**
  - Builds strong customer relationships.
  - Allows for personalized communication and persuasion.
  - Provides immediate feedback and the opportunity to address objections.
  - **Example:** Arjun's baristas became the face of his brand, using personal selling to create memorable experiences for customers who visited Bean Bliss.

- **Challenges:**
  - Can be time-consuming and expensive, especially in a retail environment.
  - Requires skilled sales personnel who can effectively communicate the brand's value.
  - **Example:** Arjun had to invest time in training his staff to ensure they could effectively represent the new blend and persuade customers to try it.

2. Advertising:

Advertising is a paid form of non-personal communication that reaches a broad audience through various media channels, such as television, radio, print, online, and outdoor ads. It is used to build brand awareness, inform potential customers, and persuade them to take action.

- **Characteristics:**
  - Broad reach, capable of targeting large audiences.
  - Controlled messaging, as the business determines the content and timing of the ad.
  - Used to create awareness, inform, and persuade.
  - **Example:** Arjun ran targeted online ads and placed posters around the city to promote his new coffee blend, reaching both local residents and tourists.

- **Advantages:**
  - Wide reach, allowing the message to be seen by a large audience.
  - Effective for building brand awareness and generating initial interest.
  - Allows for creative and visually appealing presentations of the product.
  - **Example:** Arjun's visually appealing posters, featuring the rich aroma and exotic spices of the new blend, caught the attention of passersby and intrigued them to visit Bean Bliss.

- **Challenges:**
  - Can be expensive, especially for high-impact media like television or prime online placements.
  - Less personalized than other forms of promotion, making it harder to address individual customer needs.
  - **Example:** Arjun had to carefully budget his advertising spend to ensure he got the best return on investment without overspending.

3. Sales Promotion:

Sales promotion includes short-term incentives designed to encourage immediate purchase or trial of a product. These can include discounts, coupons, contests, free samples, and other promotional offers that create a sense of urgency.

- **Characteristics:**
    - Short-term incentives designed to boost immediate sales.
    - Used to complement other promotional activities and drive action.
    - Often involves limited-time offers to create urgency.
    - **Example:** Arjun offered a limited-time discount on his new coffee blend and gave out free samples during the launch week, encouraging customers to try the product and make a purchase.
- **Advantages:**
    - Stimulates quick sales and attracts new customers.
    - Creates excitement and urgency around the product.
    - Can be easily tracked and measured for effectiveness.
    - **Example:** The buzz created by Arjun's free samples and discounts led to a spike in sales during the launch period, helping establish the new blend in the market.
- **Challenges:**
    - Can lead to short-term sales boosts without long-term customer loyalty.
    - Frequent promotions may erode brand value or lead customers to expect constant discounts.
    - **Example:** Arjun had to balance the use of sales promotions to avoid training his customers to wait for discounts rather than buying at full price.

4. Publicity:

Publicity is unpaid media coverage or word-of-mouth promotion that generates awareness and interest in a product or brand. Unlike advertising, publicity is not directly controlled by the business, making it more credible in the eyes of consumers.

- **Characteristics:**
    - Unpaid and earned, rather than paid-for.
    - Often generated through public relations efforts, such as press releases, events, or media coverage.
    - Can be highly credible and influential, as it comes from third-party sources.
    - **Example:** Arjun hosted a launch event for his new coffee blend, inviting local food bloggers and journalists, resulting in positive media coverage and online buzz.
- **Advantages:**
    - Highly credible, as it comes from independent sources.
    - Can reach a broad audience without the direct cost of advertising.
    - Builds brand reputation and trust.
    - **Example:** The positive reviews and social media posts from attendees at Arjun's launch event helped spread the word about his new blend, drawing more customers to Bean Bliss.

- **Challenges:**
  - Less control over the message and timing compared to advertising.
  - Can be difficult to generate consistently and may not always result in positive coverage.
  - **Example:** Arjun had to carefully plan his publicity efforts to ensure that the coverage was positive and aligned with his brand image.

15.3 Integrating the Promotion Mix

Kavita explained to Arjun that the key to a successful promotional strategy is integrating the various elements of the promotion mix to work together cohesively. By aligning personal selling, advertising, sales promotion, and publicity, businesses can create a consistent and compelling message that resonates with the target audience.

1. Consistency in Messaging:

Consistency in messaging ensures that the brand's message is clear, coherent, and aligned across all promotional activities. This helps reinforce the brand's identity and strengthens its position in the market.

- **Example:** Arjun made sure that all promotional materials, from posters to social media posts, used consistent messaging and visuals that highlighted the exotic flavors and premium quality of his new coffee blend.

2. Coordinated Timing:

Coordinated timing involves aligning the launch of various promotional activities to maximize impact. This ensures that the target audience receives multiple touchpoints in a short period, increasing the likelihood of engagement.

- **Example:** Arjun scheduled his advertising campaign, sales promotions, and launch event to coincide, creating a buzz around the new blend that built momentum and drove customers to his café.

3. Targeted Audience:

Targeting the right audience with the appropriate mix of promotional tools ensures that the message reaches those most likely to respond. This involves understanding customer segments and choosing the channels that will best engage them.

- **Example:** Arjun targeted coffee enthusiasts and foodies through social media ads, while also reaching casual café-goers with in-store promotions and events.

4. Measuring Effectiveness:

Measuring the effectiveness of each promotional activity helps businesses understand what works and what doesn't. This information can be used to refine future campaigns and optimize the promotion mix for better results.

- **Example:** Arjun tracked the success of his promotional activities by monitoring sales, customer feedback, and social media engagement, allowing him to adjust his strategy for future product launches.

15.4 Practical Activity: Crafting a Promotion Strategy

Activity Name: The Perfect Blend of Promotion

- **Setup:** Students will be divided into groups, and each group will create a promotion strategy for a fictional product. They will decide how to use the elements of the promotion mix—personal selling, advertising, sales promotion, and publicity—to launch the product.
- **Task:** Groups will present their promotion strategy to the class, explaining how they will integrate the various promotional tools to create a cohesive campaign. They will also discuss the target audience, timing, and expected outcomes of their strategy.
- **Presentation:** Each group will showcase their promotion mix strategy, including sample ads, sales promotion ideas, and publicity plans, followed by a class discussion on the strengths and weaknesses of each approach.

15.5 Crafting the Perfect Message

As Arjun wrapped up his exploration of the Promotion Mix, he realized that promoting his new coffee blend was about more than just placing a few ads. It was about crafting a message that resonated with his audience and delivering it through a combination of strategies that worked together to create excitement and drive sales.

With Kavita's guidance, Arjun launched a successful promotion campaign that blended personal selling, advertising, sales promotions, and publicity. By integrating these elements, he was able to create a buzz around his new coffee blend, attract customers to Bean Bliss, and establish his brand as a leader in the local coffee scene.

Arjun learned that the key to effective promotion lies in understanding the strengths of each promotional tool and using them in harmony to create a powerful, unified message. As he continued to grow his business, Arjun knew that mastering the Promotion Mix would be essential to introducing new products, engaging with customers, and driving the success of Bean Bliss.

References

- American Marketing Association. (2017). *Definition of marketing.* https://www.ama.org/the-definition-of-marketing/
- Drucker, P. F. (1954). *The practice of management*. Harper & Brothers.
- Drucker, P. F. (1973). *Management: Tasks, responsibilities, practices.* Harper & Row.
- Jobber, D., & Ellis-Chadwick, F. (2019). *Principles and practice of marketing* (9th ed.). McGraw-Hill Education.
- Kotler, P. (2003). *Marketing management* (11th ed.). Pearson Prentice Hall.
- Kotler, P., & Armstrong, G. (2018). *Principles of marketing* (17th ed.). Pearson.
- Kotler, P., & Keller, K. L. (2016). *Marketing management* (15th ed.). Pearson.
- Levitt, T. (1960). *Marketing myopia.* Harvard Business Review, 38(4), 45-56.
- Madhav, M. (2017). *The rise of Patanjali: Business and branding strategies.* SAGE Publications.
- McCarthy, E. J. (1964). *Basic marketing: A managerial approach.* Richard D. Irwin, Inc.
- Singh, S., & Verma, S. (2018). *Patanjali Ayurved Limited: Challenges and opportunities in the fast-growing FMCG market in India.* Asian Journal of Management Cases, 15(2), 166-176.
- Srivastava, R., & Prakash, S. (2015). *Patanjali Ayurveda: Emergence of a new brand.* Journal of Indian Business Research, 7(3), 245-255.
- HubSpot. (n.d.). *What is marketing?*https://www.hubspot.com/marketing-definition
- Chartered Institute of Marketing. (n.d.). *Marketing and the 7Ps: A brief summary of marketing and how it works.* https://www.cim.co.uk/media/4772/7ps.pdf
- Godin, S. (1999). *Permission marketing: Turning strangers into friends, and friends into customers.* Simon & Schuster.

www.ingramcontent.com/pod-product-compliance
Lightning Source LLC
LaVergne TN
LVHW070228170826
845679LV00035B/1871

* 9 7 9 8 8 9 6 7 3 9 0 8 1 *